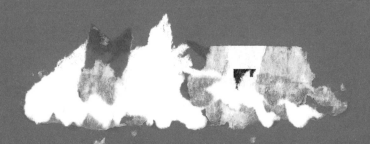

This book has feelings

Adventures in the Philosophy and Psychology of Your Mind

This 2010 edition published in the UK by:
Continuum International Publishing Group
The Tower Building
11 York Road
London
SE1 7NX

ISBN-13: 978-1-4411-9592-0

Conceived, designed and produced by Quid Publishing
Level 4, Sheridan House
114 Western Road
Hove BN3 1DD
www.quidpublishing.com

Printed and bound in China

1 2 5 7 9 10 8 6 4 2

This book has feelings

Adventures in the Philosophy and Psychology of Your Mind

Neil Scott
and Sandi Mann

continuum

contents

Chapter 1:
Your Brain on Feelings

Chapter 2:
The Evolution of Emotion

Chapter 3:
The Psychology of Emotion

Chapter 4:
Love's Emotions

Contents

what is a feeling?

One of the great joys of being a psychologist is the richness and diversity of experience. Emotions are a great example. We all have emotions but the way we experience them and our attitude toward them can differ dramatically. Some see their emotions as a great boon, the thing that makes them human and defines who they are. Others see them as a barrier to clear, effective, and rational thought.

Emotions impact every facet of our lives; but, even though we can draw on an enormous amount of psychological, historical, spiritual, and philosophical learning, we still seem to know so little about them. Emotions are such slippery things to study; we can now chart the physical changes in the brain and body that accompany emotions, but what we actually "feel" is hard to measure and communicate. Just monitoring the way I feel can change my feelings and how can I know whether "happiness" means the same thing for me as it does for you?

So, although this book reports on many of the studies and thinkers that have provided amazing insights into our emotions, don't expect to find the final, universally accepted word from the psychological community on the matter, there isn't one. It's for this reason that psychology can be so difficult and frustrating, but also so exciting, challenging, and worthwhile.

There are some big questions about emotions. Why do we have feelings? Do people have the same emotions all over the world? Are our emotions hard-wired into our biology or are they something we learn? Do our emotions affect our actions or can we change the way we feel by the way we act; for example, if you act angry, will you feel angry? And, of course, will money make you happy? You may not get all the answers here, but this book may help you enjoy thinking through the issues and arrive at some answers of your own.

But what is an "emotion" or a "feeling"? In this book, as in much of psychology, "emotion" refers to the normally quite brief physical and mental changes that occur such as happiness, sadness, anger, or fear. They are often divided into the "basic" or instinctual emotions of fear, anger, sadness, happiness, disgust, and surprise, and the "higher" or cognitive emotions such as guilt, shame, pride, and love. These higher emotions are often less immediate than the basic emotions and their causes and expression are more likely to be affected by social and cultural factors.

When we talk of "feelings" we refer to our subjective experiences of an emotion. If a bear leaps out in front of you in the woods, your heart might begin to race, your knees feel weak, you might sweat and shake, but this does not necessarily mean that you will "feel" fear. The "feeling" of an emotion is only one part of the emotional process.

A recurring theme in the book is that emotions can sometimes dominate our lives and be a source of great distress. Clearly it is advisable to consult a physician if this is the case.

One personal observation from having written this book is that reading about things like stress and depression is fascinating but can sometimes leave you feeling a little down, whereas studying, happiness and meaning can leave you feeling positive and energized. It seems so obvious, that what we immerse ourselves in will affect our emotions and mood, but perhaps not obvious enough to make us think about what we surround ourselves with. Psychology as a discipline is learning this lesson and there has been a shift in recent years to consider how we can enhance lives and increase well-being rather than just focusing so much on reducing suffering.

You can read *This Book has Feelings* from cover to cover, and this will allow you to build up your understanding of some of the fascinating things that psychologists and philosophers have discovered about the way we think and feel. Alternatively, you can just dip in and out of the book as most of the subjects don't necessarily require you to have read what comes before.

Before you begin, let's have a look at what each chapter covers.

Your Brain on Feelings describes what happens to your brain and body when you experience emotions, and how chemicals and other physical stimuli can affect the way we feel.

The Evolution of Emotion considers what the evolutionary origins or our emotions and the way we express them may be.

The Psychology of Emotion asks about the way we interpret and experience our feelings and how our actions relate to them.

Love's Emotions takes us through the ups and downs of love: why we love, how we love, and where it can all go wrong.

Fear and Excitement not only addresses why we can feel so much fear and anxiety but how these feelings help us in our daily lives and how others can use our fears.

The Angers confronts us with the many ways that we feel and express anger and helps us to examine ways of dealing with these feelings, both in ourselves and in others.

Emotions with Attitude pulls together some of the feelings that affect our health and society including how we can overcome our better emotions to do terrible things, but also how we can keep hold of hope.

Sadness and Joy explores the depths of misery and the heights of elation, asking what makes us happy and sad and what we can do to influence these feelings.

Throughout the chapters you'll find mini-features on key psychologists and other scientists who have worked in the fields discussed. Then, at the end of the book there's an index of notable psychologists, as well as a selected list of references.

Chapter 1

your brain on feelings

the emotional brain

There's something intuitively appealing about the idea that certain functions have specific locations in the brain, and to some extent this is the case. However, emotion is not located in one particular physical area but is the product of interactions between many different parts of the brain, and we are far from understanding it in all its complexity.

Structure of the Brain

The brain is classically divided into three main sections. The hindbrain and midbrain deal with basic physical functions, but the third part, the forebrain, is where our thoughts and feelings probably originate.

Most of the forebrain consists of cortex, the folded gray matter that surrounds the brain. The cortex is home to our highest functions and, although it's relatively small in most animals, it makes up about 80 percent of the human brain—a much larger proportion than for any other creature.

Where the Emotions Lie

Neuroscientist Paul MacLean has suggested that a structure called the "limbic system," also in the forebrain, is the home of the emotions. Electrical activity in this area is often accompanied by strong emotional feelings.

Located in the limbic system is the amygdala, which neuroscientist Joseph E. LeDoux has identified as the "emotional appraisal system." It's here that the decision is made whether stimuli have emotional significance or not. The amygdala is far more active when a person is presented with emotional stimuli such as sad or erotic movies, disturbing pictures, or disgusting tastes and smells.

Controlling our Emotions

Throughout history the emotions have often been viewed as inferior to thought. Many emotions have been considered more basic or raw, part of our animal nature; whereas rationality has been presented as part of our higher nature.

There is evidence to suggest that the cortex, particularly the prefrontal region where the most advanced thinking occurs, does indeed seem to inhibit and regulate our emotions. For example, cats that have had their entire cortex removed still react to fear-provoking stimuli, but they do it much faster and with less restraint. In humans, when we allow ourselves to express a genuine emotion the level of electrical activity increases in the limbic system and decreases in the cortex. However, those who have suffered damage to the prefrontal cortex often display inappropriate emotions, indiscriminately hugging and kissing strangers, or feeling proud when they have taunted people.

However, it's not simply that the cortex is rational and the limbic system emotional. The limbic system may automatically trigger emotional responses, but the cortex is where we consciously evaluate information and where we may decide (rationally) that something is scary, funny, or sad.

This may be why we are sometimes surprised by our emotions—different parts of the brain may be disagreeing about what the appropriate response is.

For example, if lesions (cuts) are made between the limbic system and frontal conscious cortex a person can appreciate that what they are seeing is horrible or scary but may not be able to feel that emotion.

Phrenology: the Search for Emotional Bumps

Phrenology was the brainchild of Franz Josef Gall and emerged in the 18th century. The rationale was that if certain faculties were located in specific parts of the brain, then the shape of the skull would mirror these facets. By "reading" these bumps one could tell whether the faculty was over- or under-developed. The iconic phrenology bust, with the various faculties mapped out on it, shows where emotions were believed to be located in the brain. The model fell into disrepute, though some practitioners can still be found.

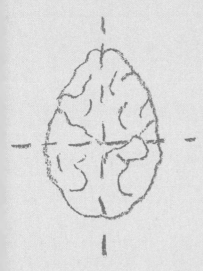

Nerves and Neurochemicals

The brain is made up of around 100 billion neurons, or nerve cells. Messages are relayed around the brain, and to and from the rest of the body, by a chain reaction of cell activation. Each cell tells the next cell along to become active (or not) by sending a chemical message, the neurotransmitter, across the gap between cells, the synapse.

These neurotransmitters play an important role in our emotions. Many emotional disorders such as mania, depression, and anxiety are associated with neurotransmitter problems. For example, having too little of the neurotransmitter serotonin is linked with depression.

the split brain

Some scientists have suggested that in effect we have not one brain, but two: one that is logical and analytical and another that is more intuitive and emotional.

The Hemispheres

The cerebral cortex is divided into two hemispheres, the right hemisphere being related to the left side of the body and vice versa. These two hemispheres have slightly different functions. For most people the left deals more with analytical and sequential tasks, as well as leading on language. The right is associated more with intuitive and emotional tasks. In a small percentage of left-handed people the hemispheric functions may be reversed.

The right-hand side appears to be better at interpreting emotional information. For example, minor musical chords sound sadder than major ones and the left ear (which connects to the right hemisphere) is better at discerning major from minor chords. When using language, the left is more concerned with grammar, words, and structure, the right with intonation and emphasis.

The hemispheres are connected by a number of nerve fibers, the most significant of which is the corpus callosum. When these connections are severed, each half has to work with only part of the information it needs.

Two Brains?

Research on those whose left and right hemispheres can no longer communicate with each other helps us understand the way that the two halves affect our emotions. Joseph E. LeDoux reports the case of P. S., who had damaged connections between his hemispheres. As with most people, his left hemisphere controlled speech, but, unusually, he could read using either hemisphere. For example, if a picture was presented to his right hemisphere, the "speaking" left hemisphere could say whether it was "good" or "bad," but could not say what was depicted. Presumably the information on what he had seen did not make it through to the left hemisphere, but the emotional judgment made by the right hemisphere did.

The emotions are not entirely held in the right-hand side of the brain, but there is good evidence to suggest that the more positive emotions are disproportionately located in the left hemisphere, the negative ones on the right.

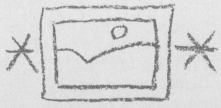

Happy or Sad?

Do this with a group of friends. You will each need a ball—a tennis ball is about the right size. Half of the group should hold it in the left hand and the other half in the right. Now everyone should squeeze the ball as tightly as possible for 45 seconds. Pause for 10 seconds and then squeeze for another 45 seconds. Repeat this until everyone has squeezed the ball four times. Without discussing it, each person should note down any emotions he or she is feeling, and score from one to ten, where one = very happy and ten = very sad.

Now compare the scores of those who held the ball in the left hand with those who held it in the right.

This is based on an experiment reported by Schiff and Lamon in 1994. They found that those who held the ball in their left hand reported feeling sad, those who held it in the right tended to feel more positive and sometimes felt more determined or assertive.

This effect is attributed to the finding that activity in the right prefrontal cortex—which is related to the left-hand side of your body—initiates more negative emotions; activity on the left, more positive ones. Those using the left hand were creating stimulation in the right hemisphere, and vice versa; this may explain why some people felt sad while others felt happier.

Mirror Image
Rather interestingly, a number of studies have shown that this left–right split also shows up when it comes to recognizing facial expressions.

People in the studies were shown images of "chimeric" faces constructed from two separate halves. One half was emotional but the other neutral. These images were paired; for example, a composite image showing the face's right side smiling and the left neutral would be placed alongside one with the left side smiling and the right neutral.

The subjects of the studies were then asked which of the images displayed the most emotion; and the one with the emotion on the left half was frequently chosen.

This is probably because the right side of your brain takes a lead in assessing emotional expressions and this side of the brain sees more of the left-hand side of each picture.

fear circuits

Not far from my home are the ranges where the British Army trains its tank gunners. Despite the "Warning! Sudden Gunfire" signs, I can still be startled when they start firing. My heart races, my muscles tense, and I feel the shock and agitation that inevitably follows someone hurling cannon shells into the next field. But this lasts less than a second before I find myself thinking "Calm down, it was just a little sudden gunfire."

There seem to be two separate responses here. One is automatic and occurs even before I know what's happening. The other is slower and takes place at a more conscious level. So what's going on?

Two Circuits?

Joseph E. LeDoux has described how there are two different circuits for responding to fear in the brain. Our first warning of fear will generally come through our senses, in this case through my ears. Having registered a sound that could signal danger, neurons start firing, and a message shoots through my nerves to my auditory prefrontal cortex. The prefrontal cortex is the more advanced part of my brain that does the conscious "thinking" and it will decide whether the sound is really something to worry about. However, thinking is a relatively slow process, in mental terms, and it's generally better for my body to get on with the business of responding to potential threats while my thoughts get themselves sorted out. So, while this information is still working its way to my prefrontal cortex, it's also taking a short cut into the part of my brain called the amygdala.

My amygdala doesn't bother with luxuries like thinking. It just sounds the alarm and starts sending messages around my body telling it to get ready for action.

Fight, Flight, or Freeze

When faced with a threat there tend to be three main responses: fight, flight, or freeze. These responses differ from creature to creature; a rabbit will generally sit very still and hope that the threat doesn't notice it, whereas a lion has a different outlook on life.

Whichever the favored response, my body is being prepared in the same way and can choose the best option for the situation. Oxygen-rich blood is pumped into the system of muscles, so I can hit harder, run faster, or hold myself very still. Sensitivity to pain is reduced so I can ignore any minor injuries that I might sustain.

This leaves me feeling a little light-headed and breathless, my muscles are tensed and time even seems to slow down. My hair stands erect to make me look bigger and scarier—impressive in a startled cat, less so in the case of human goosebumps. Defecation is another option, and researchers sometimes use the number of stools a rat deposits as an index of how scared it is. (Don't play "What's the worst job you've ever had?" with these researchers—they'll win.)

As the amygdala has been arranging all this for me, the message has reached my prefrontal cortex and I have decided whether or not this is a real threat. On this basis, I can act or I can begin to calm down. Once the threat has passed, the hormones that triggered the response dissipate and my body returns to normal. The "feeling" of fear, if experienced at all, begins to fade.

The Feedback Loop

When we are in full fear mode, our body
and mind both update each other on their
situations. If one part says it is fearful, this
helps maintain the state of fear in the other.
However, if this feedback loop is broken, it can
fundamentally alter the experience of fear.

In some cases, where people have certain
spinal injuries, the body can't get its message
of fear back to the brain. A person in a
frightening situation can be conscious of
the normal intensity of fearfulness. However,
without the body telling the mind about the
state it's in, some people report that they can't
quite "feel" the fear.

Amygdala—Home of Fear

LeDoux has dubbed the amygdala "the hub in
the wheel of fear." It receives messages from
the various parts of the brain involved in the
fear circuit and seems to be the place where
the experience is identified as "emotional."

Those undergoing brain surgery often have
to be conscious, and if their amygdala is
stimulated then they will generally report
feelings of fear. On the other hand, those with
a damaged amygdala can find it harder to
perceive both fear and anger.

the emotional child

One of the most magical moments for any parent is when a baby smiles for the first time. But is the infant really happy, or is it just a random facial expression?

The Happy Baby

Smiles often appear in the first week of life, though normally only when the baby is asleep. Waking smiles can start to happen from the second week, but it's not until the first or second month that the baby's smile starts to signal happiness when she is experiencing pleasant physical sensations. By the time she is three months old the baby finds pleasure in getting a response to her own actions, whether this is from a person or a toy (for example, one that plays a tune when touched). It's at this point that truly social smiling begins. The baby's eyes and brain are allowing her to recognize others' smiles and respond to them, and parents often notice a big change in the relationship with their baby around this point.

What Is the Baby Feeling?

So, we know when the baby is happy, but things can be less clear when she is expressing negative emotions. How can we know whether she is experiencing fear, anger, or sadness?

We generally infer babies' emotions from their facial expressions and from what initiated the emotion. For example, if we do something that we think will make the baby happy and she smiles, we assume she is happy because of this. Mothers generally believe they can identify joy, fear, interest, surprise, sadness, and anger by the time that a baby is a month old. But can they?

Psychologist Carroll Izard showed photos of babies' expressions to nurses and students and they generally agreed on what the babies were feeling. But could it be that they are all consistently wrong? For example, if I told you that people who write in capital letters are more cautious than those who do not, we could probably agree on which people, from a sample of their writing, are more cautious. Although we might agree, the relationship between caution and capital letters is one I have just invented—we would both be equally misguided.

The problem with very small babies is that, although we might agree that this one looks angry or another looks sad, their facial expressions do not always tie up with what we would expect their emotions to be at that moment. So we see what looks like sadness when we expect anger, fear when we expect sadness, and so on. One explanation is that babies' faces do not work in quite the way that adults' do. However, some psychologists believe that the emotions are not really differentiated at all at this stage; there is only a general "distress" emotion that, over time, will develop into the discrete emotions of anger, fear, and sadness. Their faces may not be giving much away so we have to rely on other cues.

The Fearful Child

Fear, like smiling, has its own pattern of development. Psychologists have found that up until about seven months, children do not generally respond fearfully to stimuli. They then become increasingly scared of a range of things such as strangers, sudden noises, and unfamiliar toys. The fear of noisy and novel toys soon disappears, but the fear of strangers increases up until about the age of two.

As they get older, children's fears turn toward monsters and scary dreams; then, about school age, they develop more everyday concerns about hurting themselves and having accidents.

Is a Baby's Temperament Stable?

Psychologist Jerome Kagan has investigated the relationship between an infant's temperament and his or her personality in later life. Some babies are easily distressed and quickly become physically aroused. They tend to be very shy and Kagan labeled them "inhibited." Those who are less easily distressed and aroused are called "uninhibited." These traits are moderately stable in early childhood, but long-term studies revealed that very highly inhibited infants tended to remain shy and in later life were more prone to anxiety. Those who were extremely uninhibited, on the other hand, were more likely to develop conduct-related problems.

However, these patterns have only been found to apply to the most inhibited and uninhibited children, and even then a child's experiences and environment can still have a major impact on how he or she turns out.

depression: a chemical matter?

When Hippocrates revolutionized medicine in the fifth century BCE, he recognized "melancholia" as one of the three main disorders of the mind, along with mania and phrenitis ("brain fever"). When despondency and sadness were of sufficient intensity to be taken for an illness, its cause was attributed to an imbalance of black bile, one of the four "humors" that regulated health.

Although Hippocrates' model has long since been discredited, the idea that physical imbalances can cause emotional illnesses such as depression has stood the test of time.

The Sad Brain

One recent revolution in helping our understanding of how brains work is Positron Emission Tomography, or PET scans. These scans allow us to see which areas of the brain become active during a given event. PET scans have identified a part of the brain's limbic system, the subgenual cingulate, as being particularly active when people are sad or suffering from depression. Nearby is a region called the anterior cingulate, which seems to be associated with optimism, but this can undergo changes after a person has had several bouts of depression.

The prefrontal cortex, the part of our brain that carries out our most complex thoughts and social interactions, is also implicated in emotions. Depressed people tend to have less activity in the left side of the prefrontal cortex and you are more likely to suffer depression if this area of your brain is damaged.

Chemical Influences

There also appear to be some chemical imbalances associated with depression. You may recall, from page 13, that neurotransmitters are the chemical messengers that one brain cell sends to another. Two of these chemicals, serotonin and noradrenaline, tend to be found in quite low concentrations in people with depression, whereas those with mania tend to have quite high levels of noradrenaline.

Many of the diverse physical and chemical treatments for depression appear to have the effect of increasing the amount of these chemicals that are available to the brain. Depriving people of their dream sleep, giving them electric shocks (see opposite), and providing more sunlight to people who feel depressed in the winter, can all have the effect of reducing depression and increasing the levels of these neurotransmitters. Furthermore, all three of the main drug types that have been successful in reducing depression increase the availability of these chemicals. Curiously, however, by the time the drugs become effective, these chemicals have often returned to the level they were at when the person was depressed.

All in the Body?

If depression can be linked to physical states, such as chemical imbalances or over-active parts of the brain, does this make the psychological therapies redundant? Far from it. Psychologist Martin Seligman has pointed out the "dirty little secret" of psychopharmacology: that the drugs and physical treatments don't cure people, they only help manage the symptoms (they are "palliatives"). Elsewhere in this book you'll discover how psychologists have identified that depressed people don't just feel different, they often think differently too. Depression often recurs and although the drugs can help cope with the illness when it happens, they don't stop it happening again. Changing the way that those who suffer from depression view themselves, and the world around them, can be an important component of managing the condition.

Electro-Convulsive Therapy

One of the most controversial medical treatments in use today is electro-convulsive therapy or ECT. With ECT, the patient receives an electric shock of 70–130 volts to the brain, leading to a seizure. But why would anyone agree to receive such a "therapy," and why would any doctor inflict it on a patient?

Developed in the early years of the 20th century by Italian duo Ugo Cerletti and Lucio Bini, ECT has been applied to a number of mental illnesses, but is most widely used in treating depression. Earlier administrations of the treatment were ugly affairs, the patient convulsing from the shocks so violently that fractured bones and chipped teeth could occur. Today, patients are anesthetized and given muscle relaxants to protect them. They generally have no recollection of the shock, though deeper memory loss and confusion can result. It's usually reserved as a last resort for severe cases after conventional psychological and drug therapies have been found ineffective. However, to those whose condition is unbearable and unremitting, ECT can provide much sought-for relief.

mood-altering drugs

We have been using drugs to alter our mental states for thousands of years but in the last 250 years we have developed the technology to synthesize more and more effective compounds. Although the medical benefits can be enormous, the euphoria and other positive feelings that many of these compounds produce has inevitably led to their use for recreational purposes. But what makes them so attractive, and why do they so often lead to dependency and addiction?

Dopamine and the Emotions

Drugs that affect the brain and spinal cord are generally referred to as "psychoactives." Much of their effect comes from their ability to stimulate or inhibit the neurotransmitters that communicate between nerve cells. It's one of these neurotransmitters in particular, dopamine, that tends to be affected by the commonly abused drugs. Like other neurotransmitters, it's released into the gap between cells (the synapse) when a nerve cell is activated. If enough dopamine is released, then the receptors in the surrounding cells will become activated too.

Dopamine is very rewarding, being most densely located in the nucleus accumbens, which some have identified as the "pleasure center" of the brain. Stimulating the dopamine systems gives you an intense sense of pleasure and euphoria, explaining the appeal of the drugs that do this.

Stimulants and Depressants

Some drugs—such as cocaine, nicotine, amphetamines, and even the caffeine we find in tea and coffee—stimulate the brain, making you feel more alert. Other drugs, such as alcohol, barbiturates, and benzodiazepines, depress certain functions of the brain, making you feel more relaxed. However, both stimulants and depressants tend to give you a feeling of wellbeing or euphoria and this is often due to the effects of dopamine. Cocaine, for example, acts by reducing the amount of dopamine that is mopped up after it has been released, so increasing the amount of the neurotransmitter that remains in the synapses.

Dependency

The great danger of all of these drugs is that they can create a dependency—a process that works like this:

The body has a natural tendency toward homeostasis; that is, the maintenance of a stable equilibrium. So, when a person starts taking a drug that stimulates dopamine production, the body will tend to compensate; something it usually does over time by reducing the impact of the dopamine, often by making the receptors less sensitive. This is what is meant by "developing a tolerance," as a person will require increasing dosages to obtain the same "hit."

Moreover, the effect of the body's adjustment can still be felt when the drug is out of the system. In the absence of the stimulating drug, a user's body returns to normal levels of dopamine; however, the system remains less receptive. Now a user will feel worse than before the drug was taken—even though he or she has a normal level of dopamine it will feel as if there is less.

Finally, there is the psychological dimension to addiction. Dopamine is such a powerful pleasure-and-reward system that the mind will focus its pleasure-seeking activities on getting whatever it was that created the rush in the first place. The mind also forges connections between the whole experience of getting the dopamine and the feeling of euphoria. For this reason, the places, equipment, even any pain involved in administering the drug all become positively associated with the emotional high, thus making it ever harder to break away.

This dependence, coupled with the need to take larger doses to produce the same effect, creates grave dangers for an addict. As well as the general risks of a drug-dependant lifestyle, the more drugs a user consumes, the greater the chance that he or she will encounter a batch of unusual purity and unwittingly administer a lethal overdose.

Of course, the increased production of dopamine is not the only thing that reinforces drug-taking habits. Cannabis, for example, has about 60 compounds that work directly on the brain, and even tea contains at least two other "psychoactives." There are also other rewards such as increased energy, reduced need for sleep, the reduction of pain, or stimulating hallucinations that various drugs offer.

As different drugs, legal and illegal, act through different mechanisms so they carry a variety of health risks. Cocaine, cannabis, and amphetamines, for example, have all been linked with psychosis, and alcohol can affect just about every organ in your body.

The Opiates

The use of opium has ancient roots. It is obtained by scoring the seed pods of the opium poppy (*Papaver somniferum*: "sleep-bringing poppy"), and collecting the resulting sap.

Opium itself is a natural and extremely effective painkiller. Its derivatives are known as opiates, and these are often more powerful than the original opium. Morphine was first extracted in 1803, and by 1896 heroin had been synthesized from it.

Opiates all promise relief from pain, feelings of euphoria and contentment, and a reduction in anxiety. They also promise very rapid addiction, which involves physical and psychological dependency, and painful and potentially dangerous withdrawal should an addict stop taking them.

carving out the emotions

It was 1935 and the Portuguese neurologist Antonio Egas Moniz was conducting some groundbreaking surgery. He drilled several holes in the head of a paranoid woman and injected pure alcohol into her brain. He was trying to destroy the connections between her prefrontal lobes, where much of our intellectual and planning activity occurs, and the rest of her brain. He reported that, following surgery, she was much calmer.

White Cut

Moniz had been inspired to try this operation by a lecture from Carlyle Jacobsen. Jacobsen described how he had turned extremely anxious and aggressive chimpanzees into calm and friendly animals using a similar procedure. Moniz developed his technique further and created a special tool for cutting the brain. He called the process leucotomy, meaning "white cut," as it severed the white matter that connects the various areas of the brain. His work in the area earned him a Nobel Prize in 1949.

The technique was originally applied to address the most severe and distressing mental illnesses including extreme depression, paranoia, and schizophrenia. However, although Moniz noted that patients were generally much calmer after the operation, they were also apathetic and disorientated, had trouble conversing, and were often incontinent.

The American Experience

Inspired by Jacobsen's lecture and Moniz's apparent success, American neurologist Walter Freeman conducted his first leucotomy in 1936. In the years that followed he reported that of 623 "lobotomies," as he now called them, over half had good outcomes, about a third were fair, and a little over 10 percent failed. Eighteen people died.

As with Moniz's operations, there was little if any long-term follow-up. Those who were operated on often lost much of their ability to plan, organize, and initiate.

The area that was destroyed linked the frontal lobes to the emotional centers in the limbic system including the amygdala and hypothalamus. As a result, the anger or despair that had brought the patient to the doctor often disappeared, but so did the ability to feel happiness, joy, and sympathy. Patients often lost the facility for expressing emotions, whether facially or by intonation, along with the ability to read the emotions of others. The knife seemed to have cut out their personalities.

Supporters of lobotomy insisted it helped those whose mental suffering or pain was intense and for whom no alternative treatment was available. However, in many cases it was applied to those with more minor symptoms or to control those whose behavior was considered a problem. It was highly controversial in its day, but its growth in popularity is probably due to the self-promotional activities of Walter Freeman.

The Ice-Pick Lobotomy

Frustrated with the limitations of the surgical approach, Freeman secretly experimented with an alternative: what has since become known as the "ice-pick" lobotomy. In this process, a small tool was inserted into the eye socket, passed through the tear duct, and then tapped to get it through the bone. It was then pushed a short distance into the brain and moved slightly to sever the nerves.

With this technique Freeman could travel around the country in his "lobotomobile" performing highly publicized lobotomies in institutions that had no operating theaters, often just using an office. Miller performed around 3,500 lobotomies himself, and overall it's estimated that over 65,000 were performed in the heyday of the technique.

With the appearance of more effective medication in the 1950s, the lobotomy became extremely rare. However, it's still practiced, albeit on a more highly regulated basis, in some countries today.

Trepanning

Moniz was not the first to use such procedures. The medical process of drilling holes in the skull, known as "trepanning," dates back as far as 5000 BCE, and was used to relieve pressure or deal with other inter-cranial problems. The recovered skulls of those who had undergone this process suggest that many survived.

The Emptiness of Agnes

The troubling nature of lobotomization, and the light that it throws upon our emotions, is underlined by case studies of those who have undergone them.

Neuroscientists Bryan Kolb and Ian Q. Whishaw have described meeting a woman called Agnes. Her face was expressionless and she showed no signs of emotion. Although she had some affection for her dogs, she had no feelings for most people or things and described herself as "empty."

She had not always been this way. She used to be very outgoing, but her husband, a wealthy businessman, was concerned that this might be a liability and persuaded two physicians to lobotomize her. She had insight into what had happened, but no feelings. In the 30 years since the operation she had had only one day of real happiness: the day her husband died.

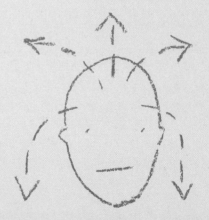

where are you in all this?

Psychologists and neuroscientists have made great progress in describing what happens in our brains, not only when we think and act but also when we feel. We know that when we feel afraid, brain cells are triggered, hormones released, and muscles and organs prepared for action. Most of this happens automatically, without our conscious input. But if fear is simply a sequence of biological actions, why do you have a subjective experience of it—where are "you" in all this?

A Continuous Self

Most people can imagine themselves set apart from their body—as a continuous person. For example, I have a memory of myself as a little boy, playing with my brother. The body, brain, enthusiasms, attitudes, and thoughts of that little boy are very different from those of the man I am now, yet I think that we are the same person and that it was me thinking that little boy's thoughts and feeling his emotions. I also believe that when I dreamed last night, even though the dream world I was in had no physical reality, it was nevertheless me who was the protagonist in the dream.

In short, I think of myself as being "someone" who is not purely my body. But am I? Am I a "soul" with a body, or am I just a body that thinks it has a soul?

Dualism

The idea that body and soul are different things is called "dualism." It has a long history, but one of its most famous proponents was the French philosopher René Descartes (1596–1650).

Descartes employed what became known as the "Method of Doubt" in a thought-experiment to find if there was anything of which he could be certain. First he reasoned that everything he experienced in the physical world could be false. Your eyes may be reading these words and your hands feel you are holding this book, but is there really a book there? What if your senses are lying? Worse, what if your hands and eyes are illusions too? Having peeled away several layers of uncertainty, Descartes concluded that there was only one thing he could be sure of: even if all else was deception there was still a "him" who was being deceived. He must therefore exist. Thus we have the most famous of all philosophical dictums: "I think therefore I am."

Our awareness of self can make dualism seem rational and attractive. It's deeply embedded in many cultures and it is this "I," this concept of a soul, that many religions teach will survive the death of our corporeal forms.

Monism

The big problem is explaining how the body and soul interact. If the soul is not physical, then how does it make the mind and body work? For example, how can my soul send adrenaline coursing through my system if it cannot touch my nerves?

Despite the efforts of countless philosophers and psychologists, this problem does not seem to go away. For many the subjective "soul'" or "consciousness" smacks too much of mysticism and spirituality. They argue that in the end we are just machines—very sophisticated ones, but machines nonetheless. This position is known as "monism."

We know, for example, that brain damage or chemicals can change the way I think or stop me having subjective feelings such as fear or joy. So, is my subjective experience purely a by-product of physical activity in my brain? Joseph LeDoux believes that all of our feelings can be explained physiologically. He has described our conscious and subjective "feelings" as "red herrings" in the study of emotion.

However, monism has its own difficulties, perhaps the greatest being the "hard problem" of consciousness. Coined by Australian philosopher David Chalmers, it's the converse of the challenge to dualism and questions how physical changes in the brain can possibly give rise to subjective experiences. In effect, if I am just a machine, how can I be aware and have feelings?

Neither of these challenges to monism and dualism have been resolved, and some believe that they cannot be. There remains the reality that we have subjective experiences, and that these are related to physical experiences; but we do not know how they join up.

Who Are You?

Suppose you woke up tomorrow morning in the body of Barack Obama. You look down and see his hands. You look in the mirror and see his face. You hear his voice muttering whatever expletives you would utter given the trauma of the situation. If you have his brain, body, and biochemistry, are you now Barack Obama, or are you still "you" but in Obama's body? The former is an approximation of the monist view, the latter the dualist view. (Although a monist might answer that such a change is impossible, even within a thought-experiment; or that if it were possible the change would go unnoticed by the individual.)

Chapter 2

the evolution of emotion

charles darwin

Charles Darwin, the British naturalist, has probably had more impact on the way we think about the world than almost any other figure in the last 250 years. Although he is best known for his work on evolutionary biology, he also laid the groundwork for much of our modern understanding of emotion and expression.

An Unlikely Scholar

Born in 1809, Charles Darwin did not appear to find study particularly rewarding and was a concern to his father, a local doctor and landowner. He often neglected his studies to pursue his interests in nature, particularly the highly fashionable hobby of beetle-hunting. He trained for the clergy but took a post aboard HMS *Beagle* in 1831 on a five-year trip to South America and the Galápagos Islands. It was in this archipelago, where he observed the differences between species, that his theories on evolution had their foundation—although it was only later that he began to develop these observations into the ideas that underpinned his theory.

Darwin's basic thesis was that the creatures weren't created as they now appear but that they evolved gradually over time. Evolution, however, was not a new theory; in fact, his own grandfather, Erasmus Darwin, had written in support of the idea before Charles was even born. But Charles Darwin's critical contribution was the idea of natural selection—the mechanism by which evolution takes place. Put simply, those offspring that are best adapted to their environment are most likely to survive long enough to breed. Their offspring are more likely to share whatever advantage the parent had, whether a long beak, opposable thumb, or sharper vision. In this way less well-adapted individuals die off while those that are better suited to meet the challenges they face, thrive.

His findings, published as *On the Origin of Species* (1859), were controversial because they implied not that we are *like* animals, but that we *are* animals. Moreover, although Darwin attempted to avoid making explicit the religious implications of his theory, the intimation that natural selection rendered God as Creator redundant offended many.

Emotional Expression

Although *On the Origin of Species* is Darwin's best-known work, he also wrote widely on other topics, including *The Expression of the Emotions in Man and Animals* (1872). Here he asks two basic questions: how are emotions expressed and where do they come from? Darwin inevitably saw a strong evolutionary component in the way we express our emotions. The "bristling of our hair" when we are frightened is the same as the reaction other animals have to fear—their hairs stand on end. Similarly, the human sneer is a remnant of the snarl, our teeth bared ready to bite. These responses are not all useful the 21st century, but they nevertheless remain part of our biology.

However, Darwin's theories on these expressions were not restricted to evolutionary causes. He also suggested that many are based on our experiences in childhood. For example, when we cry he suggests we are doing the same thing as an infant when he or she screams; we have just learnt to inhibit it a little. Where the tears of a screaming infant protect its eyes, the tears we now cry as hurt adults have no use; they are just vestiges of our infancy.

Universal Emotions

If emotional expressions are the product of evolution, then we should expect them to be universal—to be present in the wide range of different cultures. Darwin sought to find out whether this was so and mounted a major research program, sending questionnaires with photographs of different emotional expressions and all round the world, making particular use of missionaries working with remote communities. His findings were consistent with his evolutionary theory—people

of different cultures and even those who were blind from birth, so had never seen another's face, all appeared to share the same basic facial expressions.

Darwinian Research

Darwin was very aware of the difficulties in researching emotional expression. He noted that facial expressions were difficult to assess because they were so swift and the differences between expressions so slight. He was also sensitive to the way his imagination about what an expression might mean could influence his interpretations.

Adder Attack

Darwin famously recounts how difficult it is to subdue an involuntary emotional reaction. Positioned safely on the other side of a glass screen from a puff adder, he was determined not to flinch when the snake struck at him. Yet when the creature did strike he found himself leaping backward "a yard or two." His primitive reaction was stronger than his will to resist it.

Paul Ekman is one of a group of scientists who have put Darwin's theories to the test, using the technology of the 20th and 21st centuries. They routinely film expressions and work diligently through every frame noting differences. Ekman remarks that research has revealed that nearly all of Darwin's major ideas, including the universality of emotion, are supported by modern findings.

gender and emotion

There is a general belief that men and women are emotionally different. But do these differences really exist and, if so, are there real differences between the sexes or are they just a part of the way we are brought up?

The Argument for Biological Differences

The evolutionary argument runs that we have evolved in a way that maximized our chance of survival. Males needed to hunt, so aggression, spatial skills, and focus were very important. Females were more involved in the raising of children, and therefore lived a more communal life, meaning co-operation, nurturing affection, and communication were crucial.

There is a weight of evidence to support the idea that these gender differences do exist. Comparing differences on psychometric personality scales and ability tests shows that males in Western countries tend to be more dominating and decisive, are more independent, aggressive, self-assured, and analytical. Women tend to be warmer, more sociable, more sensitive to others' feelings, more conscientious, and more likely to be anxious and to worry.

But are these differences present simply because society expects males and females to operate in this way, and trains and rewards them accordingly?

There do seem to be some conspicuous biological differences in male and female brains. Female brains are more symmetrical than male brains; male brains have more neurons in the left hemisphere. There is also evidence to suggest that the corpus callosum, the main bundle of nerves that transfers information between the two hemispheres, is relatively larger in females. This suggests that male brains are more focused and analytical while female brains are more effective at multitasking.

A Communication Issue

As the genesis of feelings tends to be located more in the brain's right hemisphere, and expression in the left, could it be that men and women have the same level of emotion but that women are better able to express their emotions because of better links between the two hemispheres? When asked how emotional they have felt in the past, or how emotional they generally feel, men do report being less emotional than women. But it may be that men have been trained to think of themselves as less emotional, so asking them to reflect on how emotional they have been would make them rate themselves as unemotional in any case. However, if you ask them how emotional they're feeling right now, there's no difference between males and females.

What we know of the brain's anatomy also supports the finding that women are better than men at recognizing the overall pattern of facial and social expressions, whereas men are better at noticing specific details. Women may be more sensitive to emotions in other ways too. Research has shown that women have a much better sense of smell than men and can identify, from sweat on clothes, which people were more stressed and anxious than others.

Emotion and Status

Even with conspicuous differences in brain make-up, we do not know how much of the difference between the sexes' emotions is due to biology. Even if differences have evolved, cultures may have supported and enhanced them in a way that is not relevant to 21st-century roles. Communication and empathy seem to be valuable skills for males and females, and many of the stereotypes about, for example, what academic subjects suit males and females have to be revisited as girls increasingly outperform boys.

One conspicuous element of such emotional differences is that males tend to express more dominant and controlling emotions such as anger and pride, whereas females express more submissive or co-operative ones including fear, affection, and embarrassment. Again, there may be differences in the expression of the emotion rather than in the emotion itself. Research has shown that women are more prepared to show fear and sadness than men, but that they work harder to control emotions that might have a negative effect on relationships. Men, on the other hand, find it easier to show anger than women, and they tend to control the emotions that might diminish their power.

What We Expect to See

We all have expectations of the type of emotion that males and females demonstrate, and a number of studies by cognitive psychologist D. Vaughn Becker and colleagues at Arizona State University have delved into the effects of this.

Their research showed that when presented with a selection of male and female faces showing anger or happiness, respondents recognized both angry male and happy female faces more quickly than either angry female or happy male faces.

Further studies looked at this from another angle, presenting people with androgynous faces and asking them to identify the faces as male of female. The result was that people more readily identified angry faces as male and happy faces as female.

These and other findings underline just how strong the link between gender and the perception of emotion can be.

do animals share our emotions?

My wife sometimes worries that our dog is depressed. Lying there sighing, with a long face and doleful eyes, she does indeed look sad and weary. But she looks exactly the same to me when she is chasing a rabbit or eating. Maybe it's just that type of face. But how can we tell what she is feeling, or even if she is feeling anything at all?

Animals Obviously Have Feelings...

At one level it seems obvious that animals have feelings. If you shout at a cat it backs away, its hair on end and its eyes staring. At other times, sitting on your lap and purring as you stroke it, it seems very content. Animals seem to present the emotional behaviors that we would expect them to, given the situation they're in.

Physiologically we know that mammals, at least, have similar brain structures to our own and much of our research into human emotions begins with experiments on animals. If we scare a rat its fear centers are stimulated, neurotransmitters and hormones released, and muscles activated much as we would expect our own to be.

The theory of evolution suggests that our own emotional systems have developed from those of animals, providing further support for the idea that their experience must be at least similar to ours.

...But What Kind of Feelings?

The main problem is that we're mentally very different from other animals and we don't know what emotions mean to any given animal or whether it has a subjective experience of them. Our prefrontal cortex, thought by many to be the home of consciousness, is dramatically more developed than that of any other creature. We are also the only ones to have natural language, without which many psychologists believe consciousness to be impossible.

Some psychologists suggest that emotions affect animals in the same way as they might affect a robot. If the robot entered a dangerous situation it might send messages around its circuits to prepare itself to cope with the danger while signaling a warning to other robots. But it would not have any subjective feeling of distress, just a set of behavioral responses to danger.

Think Like a Dog

Even if animals have consciousness, it's probably something very different to ours. Imagine a dog's perception of the world. You might be tempted to see it as a variation of our own. For example, you might expect it to experience hunger in the same way as you or I do, simply with different targets for its hunger—it likes offal, you might prefer cake. But it probably isn't that simple. Your cortex allows you to think about past foods, future foods, and even social and presentational aspects of your meals. You can imagine the taste, and express and develop those thoughts and feelings in words to further excite yourself. The dog probably doesn't have the mental apparatus to do all of this, and may simply be mechanically responding to a basic drive.

The dog's world is so different from ours that we can no more comprehend it in our terms than we can describe colors to people who have never seen them.

So how can we tell? Some psychologists have tried the "rouge test," putting a mark on a creature's face and then putting the creature in front of a mirror to see if it will try to remove the spot, which it can only do if it is self-aware and realizes the reflection is of itself. It seems that chimpanzees and orang-utans can pass the test, but other primates can't. Cats and dogs fail miserably.

Even here we don't know whether an animal is aware that the reflection represents itself (and so has an awareness of itself as separate) or if it's just a cue about the animal's environment. Normally we can't ask it, the exception being that the only gorilla we know of who has passed the rouge test, Koko, had been taught sign language. When asked who was in the mirror she signed "me, Koko." However, her limited vocabulary and comprehension mean we can't necessarily infer from this that she is fully aware.

The simple answer to the question about animal emotions is that we don't know. The evidence strongly suggests that animals will have the same responses to stimuli that we have, but we do not have any solid evidence to say whether or not they actually have a subjective feeling of fear, anger, or happiness.

facial expressions

We probably take it for granted that if someone is smiling he or she is happy, and if a person frowns it is because he or she is angry. But can we really assume that everyone uses the same expressions to convey the same feelings?

Culture or Evolution?

Darwin believed that many of our facial expressions come from our biology and that they should therefore be broadly the same around the world. The work of psychologist Paul Ekman and his colleagues supports this view. However, there are many elements of expressions that do differ from one culture to the next.

Some of our facial expressions seem to be more or less out of our control and so are less affected by cultural factors. When we are interested in something or attracted to someone our pupils dilate, and there is not a great deal we can do about it. In fact, photographs of people can be made to look more attractive by increasing the size of the pupils—we all like someone more if they seem to like us, even if we're not sure why we think they like us!

However, a universal expression is often modified by cultural norms. Westerners use eye contact to manage conversations and show interest, but in some cultures eye contact is avoided as a sign of respect. In some Asian contexts it's interpreted as a competitive gesture.

Facial Control

One of the main ways that culture affects expressions is in how openly and fully they are displayed. There has been much interest in the difference between individualist cultures, where the focus is on the individual, and collectivist cultures, in which group membership is more central.

This was studied in an experiment by Ekman, in which he compared the reactions of Japanese subjects, from a collectivist culture, and Americans, whose culture is more individualistic, to a film. When viewing the film entirely alone, both nationalities showed the same facial expressions, but when there was an observer present the expressions of the Japanese subjects were more muted.

Try This with Some Friends

The next time you're planning to watch a funny television program, get some pencils ready. At the beginning of the show, half of the group should hold a pencil between their teeth and the other half should hold it tightly in their lips. After five minutes, everyone should take the pencils out and independently rate how funny the program was on a scale of one to ten.

This mimics a 1988 study by Strack, Stepper, and Martin, which found that people who hold the pencil in their teeth are more likely to find the show funny. This is thought to be because the act of holding the pen between the teeth forces the face into a "smiling" position, whereas holding the pen between the lips creates a "frown."

This provides support for the idea that the expressions we make affect our mood, rather than simply being a product of it.

Next time you're feeling glum, put on a smile. It might just cheer you up.

This suggestion that Japanese people regulate their expressions more was supported by the work of David Matsumoto and his colleagues. They found that when shown the same emotional expression, Japanese people attributed less emotional intensity to it than Americans did. The Japanese assumed that the amount of emotion being expressed was the amount of emotion that the person felt, but Americans were more likely to say that the expression overstated what the person was actually feeling.

Further, although Americans and Japanese were equally good at recognizing positive emotions, for example, happiness and surprise, the Americans were better at recognizing negative emotions such as anger, disgust, fear, and sadness, perhaps because they are more available in that culture.

Landis's Lab Rats

A rather gruesome footnote to the body of research into facial expressions is Carney Landis's infamous 1924 experiment. Landis, a postgraduate at the University of Minnesota, set out to determine whether different facial expressions were specific to particular emotions; in other words, whether different people would display the same expression when they were made to feel the same emotion.

Landis's subjects, who were mostly students, had their faces painted with black lines to highlight their facial expressions, and Landis proceeded to photograph them as they responded to each particular stimulus. To start with, these were relatively benign: he instructed subjects to smell ammonia, look at pornography, and place their hand in a bucket of frogs. But the test had a grisly climax.

Participants were given a live white rat and instructed to decapitate it. They initially resisted, but after a while two-thirds did it; worse, they did it badly and the rats suffered greatly. In the cases of the remaining third who refused, Landis would do it while they watched.

Landis, however, was unable to prove his hypothesis. His study remains more famous as an example of what people will do when told to by an authority figure (see pages 146–7), than for any insight gained into facial expressions.

paul ekman

American psychologist Paul Ekman (b. 1934) has spent a career exploring the importance of facial expressions. In a postwar climate where the focus was firmly on cultural explanations for many psychological phenomena, he revitalized interest in Darwin's belief that emotional expressions were determined primarily by evolution. He has also pioneered the use of a range of techniques to identify when people are lying.

Expressions of the World

Ekman and his colleagues set out to test Darwin's theory that facial expressions are universal, and reduced his arguments to two basic hypotheses:

1. The "encoding hypothesis" states that if emotional expressions are universal then the same feeling should give rise to the same expression in different cultures.

2. The "decoding hypothesis" states that if the same expression is shown to people from different cultures they should agree on what feeling the face is expressing.

Ekman began by showing photographs of facial expressions to people from different countries. He used the six basic expressions of anger, fear, surprise, happiness, sadness, and disgust. People from Argentina, Brazil, China, Japan, and the United States were shown the photos, and there was 80–90 percent agreement on which of the six feelings each photo represented.

However, people from these countries had all been exposed to American films and media, so could have learned a shared meaning of what these responses meant. Ekman therefore took the photos to the Fore, a remote group of Papua New Guineans who had remarkably little contact with Westerners. Here too there was 80–90 percent agreement; a finding that suggests that these expressions are universal. Ekman also recorded the expressions of the Fore, and U.S. college students were able to identify the emotions they were expressing.

Ekman also found it was easier to judge an expression from video than from photos. This is probably because many of the components of an expression are fleeting and subtle.

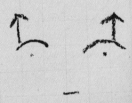

...e Diogenes Project

...hen Ekman and his ...lleague William Friesen ...d created their "facial ...tion coding system," which ...scribed the make-up of ...ch expression, they noted ...at we cannot voluntarily ...ntrol some of our facial ...uscles. That's why it's so ...rd to convincingly fake ...me expressions.

...we can't fully control our ...cial muscles and our ...notional expressions, could ...ur expressions give us away ...hen we are lying? According ... Ekman and his associate, ...aureen O'Sullivan, they ...an. They have explored ...nicroexpressions," very ...rief involuntary expressions ...e make when we are trying ... hide what we are truly ...inking and feeling. When ...ou combine the content of ...hat someone is saying with ...eir body language and ...ese microexpressions, it can ...ive you a good insight into ...hether someone is telling ...e truth.

Ekman and O'Sullivan set up the Diogenes Project to test the theories out and identify people who were particularly good at spotting liars. Having tested 20,000 people, they identified 50 of these "truth wizards." These people seem to be naturals at detecting liars, though one of the main things they have in common is that they work hard at it. O'Sullivan reports that attorneys and secret service agents appear to do quite well in this area, but gender and education have not emerged as a factor.

The project has attracted a lot of attention and it's claimed that, using their findings, you can improve your ability to spot a liar in just 20 minutes. There is even a television series, "Lie To Me," about a team that uses applied psychology to solve mysteries, and the lead character is based on Paul Ekman.

The Split-Brain Lie Detector

Nancy Etcoff and colleagues at Harvard University have found that people with damage to their left hemispheres are better at spotting liars than people with right brain damage. This should not be too surprising because, as we saw in the first chapter, the right hemisphere of the brain is more involved in reading emotional expressions than the left. However, they also seem to be better at spotting liars than those who have both left and right hemispheres functioning. Etcoff puts this down to the right brain attending more to the expression, while the left brain can too easily be misled by words.

...pot the Expression

...kman found that not all expressions are equally easy to identify; for example, happiness is ...elatively easy to recognize, but people often find it harder to discriminate between fear and ...urprise. Nevertheless, in 1972, he put forward a list of six basic emotions: anger, disgust, fear, ...appiness, sadness, and surprise. Then, during the 1990s, Ekman expanded his model, proposing ...hat amusement, contempt, contentment, embarrassment, excitement, guilt, pride in achievement, ...elief, satisfaction, sensory pleasure, and shame were also universal in nature.

embarrassment: a matter of culture?

If our emotions are the products of evolution, what possible purpose could embarrassment have served?

Knowing Your Place
The Canadian sociologist Erving Goffman (1922–82) suggested that blushing and bowing your head was once a way of signaling submission to a superior. It showed that you knew where you stood and weren't a challenge, so didn't need to be attacked.

As it's a social emotion, you shouldn't be able to experience embarrassment until you're self-aware and can distinguish yourself from those around you.

There is a simple test for this called the "rouge test," which we've already seen on page 35. A spot of rouge is put on a child's forehead without her knowledge. The child is then put in front of a mirror. If she is able to touch the rouge then this demonstrates the understanding that the image in the mirror is her own.

Children do not generally exhibit embarrassment until they are able to "pass" the rouge test.

Expressing Embarrassment
The psychologist Dacher Keltner examined film of embarrassed people, frame by frame, to identify the components that make up the expression of embarrassment. (Keltner has been very creative in finding ways of eliciting embarrassment—he seems particularly proud of getting students to sing Barry Manilow's "Feelings" in a dramatic manner.)

Within the first three-quarters of a second the eyes look down, then the head turns (usually left) and moves down, all within the next half-second. There is usually a smile—quite controlled, with lots of lip movement including puckering, pursing, and sucking—which lasts around two seconds. There will usually be two or three furtive upward glances and some touching of the face.

A Matter of Respect

Keltner has tested the idea that embarrassment is a way of showing submissiveness and deference. He asked ten-year-old boys a series of questions that were too hard for them to answer. Well-adjusted children tended to show embarrassment at not being able to answer, whereas more aggressive boys did not. He concluded that embarrassment signals a respect for others and that we know and are prepared to abide by the rules.

Having established that people recognized these expressions as embarrassment, Keltner then tried to identify similar patterns in the animal world, with some success. Gaze aversion is a classic way for animals to cut off an aggressive encounter, and the head movements are quite common in submissive primates. In submission, both primates and rabbits try to hide their faces and this may be the origin of human face-touching.

Cultural Factors

The specific causes of embarrassment, and the way it's expressed, vary from one culture to the next.

The key components of the embarrassed expression, as described above, appear to be quite universal, but in Southeast Asia, shrugging the shoulders and holding the tongue between the teeth are also incorporated. Such additional cues do not translate as well as the basic ones; although over 50 percent of Indians recognized this as a sign of embarrassment, only around 10 percent of Americans did.

Nevertheless, the shoulder shrug is a particularly effective submissive gesture—raters judge a person as being physically smaller when he or she is shrugging than when displaying anger.

Some societies—for example, southern European and South American ones—freely show their emotions, whereas others such as the English and Japanese tend to put more emphasis on emotional restraint. For example, becoming angry in a business meeting in Japan might signal rudeness or a lack of control, whereas in Spain it might be questioned why a person who was clearly angry was trying to hide their emotions.

In emotionally controlled countries, a public display of emotion can be a cause of great embarrassment. For example, the Japanese have a particular social phobia called *jin-kyofu-sho*—the fear of embarrassing others. In America, in contrast, social phobias focus more on being subject to the judgment of others.

The Blush

The blush, a reddening of the face and ears when embarrassed, ashamed, or shy, doesn't seem to be unique to humans. Darwin believed it was caused because blood flows to whichever part of the body a person is focusing on. When embarrassed, you feel very exposed and so blood flows to your face.

Research suggests that the blush is more likely to occur when you are embarrassed than in other emotional states.

the psychology of disgust

At some levels disgust appears to be one of the emotions with the most obvious evolutionary causes. Revulsion at rotten food or the signs of disease seems quite fundamental to our preservation. Yet closer examination shows disgust to be very culturally defined.

Core Disgust

Disgust is an easily recognized emotion. The wrinkled nose, raised upper lip, and slightly open mouth are universal, and the facial expression itself seems to reveal the function of the emotion: the sense of taste and smell are protected and the slightly open mouth and protruding tongue are ready to expel something unpleasant.

Jonathan Haidt, Paul Rozin, Clark R. McCawley, and their colleagues note that there are three obvious sources of disgust: bad food, bodily products (such as feces and vomit), and some animals. They refer to these as the elements of "core disgust," and it seems likely that they developed to protect us from contamination. However, Haidt's colleagues tell us that this is only one of several areas of disgust; there is so much more to be disgusted by.

Spend a minute thinking of the things that really disgust you. Notice while you're doing it that you can distinguish those things that scare you or that you merely dislike from those that disgust you because, with the latter, you may find yourself wrinkling your nose and raising your upper lip in disgust.

When asked to consider what is disgusting, many people think of taboo sexual acts, poor hygiene, things related to death (including corpses), and body damage such as gore and open wounds. Haidt and his colleagues suggest that what these have in common is that they all remind us of our animal nature and so they reveal our mortality. Disgust protects us from confronting these things and Haidt and colleagues call it "the guardian of the temple of the body." The only bodily products that people don't tend to feel negative about are tears, which are also the only one that people think of as unique to humanity.

Moral Disgust

When Haidt's colleagues asked Americans and Japanese to list what most disgusted them, only about 25 percent of what they came up with related to core disgust, and Americans and Japanese gave similar responses in this area. However, they differed significantly on the types of moral acts they found disgusting. The Americans were most disgusted by violence against vulnerable individuals, particularly where the victim's dignity was undermined. The Japanese subjects related more day-to-day interactions that involved routine social injustices. This seems to reflect America's cultural concern with the rights of the individual to autonomy and independence, as opposed to the collectivist Japanese focus on maintaining appropriate group relationships.

Learning to Be Disgusted

Does this cultural element only apply to moral disgust? It seems obvious that disgust at bad food and body products protects us from poison and disease, yet animals and infants have no such reservations. Scavengers will happily devour rotten meat and excrement, and children may be disgusted by the bitter taste of healthy vegetables, but not by the sight of feces. Culture also plays a role. The rich cheeses that many Europeans favor smell rotten and look diseased to the uninitiated; and in some cultures kissing is considered disgusting. Even the link between cleanliness and disease is a relatively modern discovery; the British Army had an edge over many of its enemies because it was one of the first to realize that placing the latrines outside a camp resulted in much lower rates of disease among the troops.

Hitler's Sweater

Would you wear Hitler's sweater? We seem to have a strong model of contamination in our thinking about disgust that overrules our reason. People are reluctant to eat food that has been touched by a cockroach even though the cockroach has been sterilized and is therefore free of disease. Haidt and his colleagues found that people's reluctance to wear clothes that have been worn by someone else is much stronger if the person has had a misfortune, such as losing a leg, or if they're perceived as a bad person. Hitler's sweater emerged as the item people would be most reluctant to wear, as though his evil were contagious.

What we find disgusting ourselves can change quickly with exposure—the first diaper I changed was quite disgusting but I soon got used to it. Perhaps evolution merely prepared us to be disgusted. Could the rest simply be what we learn?

Chapter 3

the psychology of emotion

but how do you really feel?

How good are we at understanding exactly what emotion we are experiencing? What we call an "emotion" is actually an interaction between a range of processes—some physical (in our bodies) and some cognitive (in our minds). For example, we might experience "butterflies" in the stomach when we feel anxious, but feel sick when we're frightened. In fact, quite a lot of the bodily changes do not differ that much between emotions and it is only when our brains get involved that we're able to label what we're feeling as "fear" or "excitement."

Catching the Bus

Imagine yourself in the following scenarios:

1. You're walking briskly down the road toward the bus stop. The bus is due in about a minute and you should just make it. As you get a bit closer, you see the people at the stop start to stand up and gather their belongings. You realize that the bus must be approaching and you start to run. If you miss this bus, there will be a 15-minute wait for the next one. You run faster as you dash across a road, and your heart rate starts going up. After a few more seconds running, you start to feel hot and feel sweat trickling down the back of your legs. Another few seconds and you are panting and gasping for breath. Your legs start feeling weak as if they cannot carry you any farther.

2. You're walking briskly down the road toward the bus stop. The bus is due in about a minute and you should just make it. As you get a bit closer, you see the people at the stop start to stand up and gather their belongings. You realize that the bus must be approaching and you start to run. If you miss this bus, there will be a 15-minute wait for the next one. You run faster as you dash to cross a road, when a truck suddenly squeals into your path. You trip in your frantic efforts to escape but as you anticipate the terrible crunch of the impact, the truck screeches to a halt just before it hits you. The driver swears at you as you scramble up and onto the safety of the sidewalk. He drives away and you realize that your heart is pounding. You feel breathless and hot. Sweat is pouring down your face. Your legs feels weak and buckle as you sit down on the sidewalk.

Author's Comments

Both situations result in the same physical sensations, but you are likely to interpret these bodily changes differently in each scenario; the first as a response to exercise and the second as an emotion, in this case fear.

The same physical experience can actually be labeled in different ways by our brain—depending on what preceded the physical sensations. So, if someone threatens us, we "feel" fear; if we've just learned that we have won the lottery, we "feel" joy. Our brain helps us make sense of what our bodies "feel" by placing these feelings into some sort of context. These feelings can even, as the thought-experiment opposite illustrates, be ascribed to a non-emotional source such as physical exercise, if it's a plausible explanation.

Emotional Range

The range of emotions that we can experience is very wide, with some emotions being "basic"—that is, hard-wired into our brains, or innate. These are the emotions that most people across different cultures both experience and recognize; they include such feelings as love, hate, anger, disgust, and surprise. Show anyone anywhere in the world a picture of someone expressing one of these and the chances are he or she will know what the person is feeling right away. Other emotions are thought to be learned, culturally specific, or even combinations of "basic" emotions—such feelings as disappointment, anticipation, contempt, and jealousy. These emotions are much harder to recognize, both in others and by those who are experiencing them.

Of course, not everyone reacts to emotions in the same way. People with autism, for example, find it hard to "read" emotions and this can impair their ability to communicate. Such people can benefit from special training programs to help them recognize emotional expressions in human faces.

there is no emotion, but thinking makes it so

Emotion isn't always the result of noticing physical changes in our body and giving these emotional labels. Quite often, an emotion is the consequence of the way we interpret or explain the world around us. This explains why the same thing can happen to two people who then experience two totally different emotions as a consequence. It's our cognitive appraisal of the event that makes all the difference, as the thought-experiment below shows.

What Do You Feel?

1. Your colleague gets a promotion at work. You wanted that promotion and felt you deserved it more than her. What emotion do you feel?

2. Your colleague gets a promotion at work. It was a promotion that you really didn't want because of all the extra admin and longer working hours involved. What emotion do you feel?

3. You're waiting to be served in a bank. There is a long queue and you're using up your precious lunch hour. You get to the front but the checkout clerk pulls down the blind and tells you this desk is "out of service" now. What do you feel?

4. You're waiting to be served in a bank. There is a long queue and you're using up your precious lunch hour. You get to the front but the checkout clerk suddenly starts coughing and choking. She starts going red in the face and pulls down the blind, indicating to you that this desk is "out of service" now. What do you feel?

5. You're waiting to meet a potential client at her workplace and are kept waiting for 15 minutes. No apology is offered. You have very little choice but to sit there and re-read your notes over and over again. How do you feel?

6. You're waiting to meet a potential client at her workplace and are kept waiting for 15 minutes. You're brought a coffee by an apologetic secretary and pass the time reading quality newspapers supplied in the waiting area. How do you feel?

How Does Appraisal Work?

According to a study conducted by Arnold Lazarus in 1982, the appraisal process can be divided into two main sub-processes:

1. **Primary appraisal:** This is where we notice an event, circumstance, or situation and classify it as either positive, negative, or totally irrelevant to our wellbeing. Within this process, we have to ascertain how much the event affects (or is likely to affect) our goals or commitments.

2. Secondary appraisal: Now, we look at ourselves to see what resources we have to cope with the event or situation that we have noticed. Here, we might look at whether there is something that can be done to change what has happened, or whether we should be looking to blame someone for what has happened.

According to cognitive appraisal theory, it is the difference in the appraisal outcomes that affects which emotion we experience. For example, when we ascribe blame to someone else during secondary appraisal, we might feel anger, but if we blame ourselves, we might feel guilt. This is why the same event (for example, failing a driving test) can produce different emotions (in this example, guilt at wasting money spent on lessons, or anger at an over-zealous driving instructor).

Unconscious Processing

Cognitive appraisal happens at a subconscious level and is usually instantaneous. One experiment to support this theory involved presenting participants with quick flashes of emotion-laden words—the exposure was so short that the participants were not even aware of the presence of the words. And yet participants who were subjected to negative words such as "war" or "cancer" reported a more negative mood than those who were exposed to more positive words such as "music" or "friends."

These processes can be used by advertisers, marketers, and others who want to persuade us to their way of thinking. By inducing a positive mood in subtle ways at the unconscious level, they can influence our buying patterns (since we are more likely to want to repeat an experience that we associate with making us feel good).

Cognitive appraisal at a conscious level can also be used by clinicians to treat depressed people; by helping them to reappraise what happens in their lives, patients can learn to restructure their perceptions of things that happen to them in a more positive way.

william james and walter cannon

Psychologists and philosophers have been grappling with the issue of exactly what an emotion is for well over a hundred years. William James and Walter Cannon were among the first to devise the now-classic theories to explain how we feel emotions.

William James

Psychologist William James first outlined his theory of emotion in the journal *Mind* in 1884. Actually, he only just beat Danish physician Carl Lange to it, as they both postulated that the same processes were involved. Consequently, the resulting theory is referred to as the "James-Lange theory of emotion," acknowledging the input of both parties.

Their proposal was that emotion occurs as a direct result of physiological changes produced by the autonomic nervous system (the part of the nervous system that governs involuntary actions). Your autonomic nervous system causes physical changes to occur in your body in response to sensory input. You then interpret those changes as an emotion. For example, a grizzly bear approaches you in the woods. This external stimulus causes your heartbeat to increase and your legs to tremble. You notice these changes in your body and decide that you must feel frightened. ("I am trembling, therefore I am frightened.")

This theory turned on its head what was seen as the obvious sequence of events at the time. As James himself said, "Common sense says, we lose our fortune, are sorry and weep; we meet a bear, are frightened and run; we are insulted by a rival, are angry and strike." This, he claimed, was the incorrect order of events; actually we feel sorry because we cry, we're angry because we hit, and we're afraid because we tremble. Without the physical reactions in our bodies, we might take a rational course of action to, for example, run away from the bear, but this would be an unemotional, cognitive decision, devoid of any feeling—we would not actually feel frightened unless we experienced the physical changes first.

This theory has largely been discredited. It was first challenged by Walter Cannon in the 1920s, who reversed the sequence of events postulated by James totally.

Walter Cannon

Cannon (who was later joined by Phillip Bard) disagreed with the James-Lange theory and put forward four main arguments to refute it:

1. People can, in fact, experience physiological arousal without experiencing emotion; for instance, when they have been engaged in exercise. In this case, the physiological symptoms, such as increased heart rate, are not indicative of emotions (see page 46).

2. Physiological reactions happen quite slowly, so are unlikely to be the cause of the experiences of emotion, since we often experience emotions quite quickly. For example, if you are alone at night in your house and hear a sudden suspicious noise, you are likely to feel afraid rather quickly, while the physical "symptoms" of fear generally take longer to materialize.

3. People can experience very different emotions even when they have the same pattern of physiological arousal. For example, a person may have an increased heart rate and feel breathless both when he is angry and when he is excited.

4. Emotion was still found to occur even when the physical changes occurring in the body could not be communicated back to the brain. Cannon conducted experiments on cats in which he disconnected the nerves giving feedback to the brain—these cats still demonstrated "rage" when provoked (this was called "sham rage" because, according to Lange, without feedback to the brain, they shouldn't experience real rage at all).

The Cannon-Bard theory of emotion, as it became known, suggested that, rather than the physical reactions coming first and then producing the emotion, the two processes happen simultaneously. Emotions originate from the hypothalamus in the brain. Some external stimulus (such as the sight of a bear) will trigger the thalamus to send information simultaneously to both the brain (specifically the cerebral cortex) and the autonomic nervous system (including the skeletal muscles) so that both the awareness of emotion (in the brain) and the physical reaction (such as in the muscles), occur at once.

feeling and emotion influence perception

Can emotions actually enhance our perception? It seems that they can; and fear is especially good at making our perceptions all the more heightened. A study in 2006 showed that participants who were primed to be "fearful" were more sensitive to visual contrast. Emotional reactions, then, seem to send our visual cortex into overdrive.

Perceptual Defense

Many researchers certainly believe that our emotional state can effect our perceptions of the world around us. For example, there is a psychological phenomenon termed "perceptual defense" that nicely demonstrates how our emotions can influence our perceptions. Experiments have shown that subliminally perceived words (words that we are not consciously aware of having perceived) that evoke unpleasant or negative emotions take longer to perceive at a conscious level than neutral words.

In 1949 Elliott McGinnies showed this by having participants read words out. Some of the words presented to them were emotionally neutral (such as "apple," "glass," and so on) but others were emotionally arousing, "taboo" words (such as "penis" and "whore"). The participants were timed to see how long it took them to read the word out loud, and the results revealed that it took longer for subjects to name the taboo words. It was suggested that the reason is that our perceptual systems somehow defend us against being upset or offended by not recognizing emotionally negative events as quickly as emotionally non-arousing events.

A similar study by Halberstadt *et al* in 1995 showed that if participants were asked to quickly jot down words that were read out to them, they were more likely to write "presents" than "presence" if they were feeling happy. On the other hand, if they were feeling sad, they were more likely to perceive the word "band" as "banned."

Practical Implications

The way our emotions influence our perceptions can be seen in many aspects of everyday life. For example, if we are bored, we perceive time to pass more slowly than if we are enthusiastic (hence the saying, "Time flies when you're having fun"). A study by Jeanine Stefanucci and Justin Storbeck at the University of Virginia has shown that emotional arousal can even elevate our perception of height such that we perceive buildings to be taller after being shown emotionally arousing images. This could help explain why people with phobias might experience the world differently from those who are not phobic; it could be that their increased fear makes them perceive things to be more extreme (taller, more dangerous, and so on). Emotional arousal can intensify evaluations of a situation so that when we're afraid, we perceive things as more extreme.

Imagine This!

Imagine a balance beam like the ones used in gymnastics. Imagine that it is placed on the ground. Can you walk across it? Of course, no problem!

Now imagine that the same beam is at waist height. Can you still walk across it? Probably, though with a little more care.

What if the plank were stretched across a deep gorge? Most of us wouldn't dare go near it, even though the act of walking along it and maintaining balance should be no more difficult than when it was on the ground.

Author's Comments

This thought-experiment, adapted from one by cognitive scientist Don Norman, underlines the strange things that happen when perspective interacts with emotion. Why would a simple task suddenly become so difficult—impossible, even? You can tell yourself all you want that if you can walk on the beam on the ground, you can still walk on it across that gorge. But you still won't walk along it. Fear dominates and changes our perceptions of what we are capable of doing.

Our Emotions Affect Pain

Our emotional states can also affect how we perceive pain, with negative emotional states leading to higher perception of pain that positive ones. For example, research has shown that depressed cardiac patients experience more pain from the same angina than non-depressed ones. Within dentistry, it has been shown that anxious patients report more post-operative pain than less anxious patients. Inducing a positive mood with pleasant music or funny films can thus reduce the perception of pain—strategies that a 2008 study published in the *Journal of the Canadian Dental Association* found many dentists would be wise to implement in their surgeries.

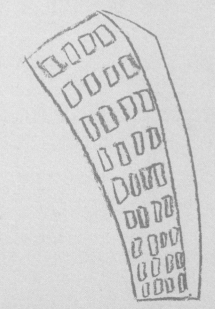

mood and memory

When we encode a memory, we not only record the visual and other sensory information, we also store our mood and emotional state alongside it. This is why a certain scent such as newly mown grass can make us feel happy; the memory of that scent is tied in with the feelings of happiness experienced at that time—perhaps during childhood picnics on summer days.

Not only do sensory stimuli evoke the moods associated with them when they were encoded in our memories, the opposite is true too. Our current mood can also evoke memories that were encoded alongside those moods. Thus, when we feel happy, it is easier to recall good memories, but when we feel sad or depressed, we're more likely to recall the bad times. This is why when we're happy, everything suddenly seems great in the world, but when something bad happens it seems that our whole world is falling apart. This phenomenon of memory linked with mood is termed "affective congruence," or "mood-congruent memory."

So, if you want to remember something from your past, try to get yourself into the mood you were in when you experienced the event.

Rainy Days

It might not seem like rocket science to discover that our mood is often better on a lovely sunny day than a cold, rainy one, but it seems that this mood affects our memories too. Studies by Joseph Forgas and colleagues have shown how the weather can affect our memory via its effects on our mood.

The researchers employed the help of a newsagent's shop in Sydney, Australia. They tested the ability of 73 shoppers to recall ten objects, such as toy cars, that were placed around the counter. The shoppers were quizzed after they left the store, with half of them tested on rainy, cloudy days and the others tested on bright, sunny days.

A mood questionnaire confirmed that the moods of shoppers tested on rainy days were worse than those tested on sunny days. And the memory test showed that rainy-day shoppers correctly identified three times as many items as the participants tested on a sunny day. The reason for this could be that a bad mood triggers a more skeptical, careful mode of processing, in contrast to the less vigilant, conceptual thinking style that characterizes a better mood.

This has implications for a range of practical applications. One might be that students wanting to recall material for exams might do better by saving the really hard stuff for a rainy day!

Try This: Music and Emotions

Select any piece of music from your CD collection. It can be classical, pop, folk, jazz … whatever. Play a couple of minutes and as it plays, write down any emotions that you associate with the music as you feel them. For example, you might start off with a bouncy piece that makes you feel upbeat and summery—a "holiday" mood. The piece might then change timbre and make you feel pensive before moving you into a more reflective mood.

How does music have such power over our emotions? Advertisers are well aware that certain pieces of music will inspire desired emotions when played alongside their products—they use this transference effect to transfer that emotion to their product. Cinema music too is used with great effect to stimulate appropriate moods in the audience. Background music is used in shops and even

casinos to encourage people to linger; or in fast-food restaurants to encourage people to eat faster! Music therapy is used to help heal not just physical problems but mental health issues too.

Part of the reason that music influences emotions so much is to do with memory. It is thought that music is processed in the emotional part of the brain, the amygdala, and thus, musical memories have strong emotions attached to them. But really the whole music–emotion connection is still a mystery to scientists. They do know, however, that music can lower the stress hormone cortisol, raise levels of melatonin (associated with sleep), and affect the release of endorphins (our body's natural painkillers). So, next time you feel stressed, can't sleep, or are in pain (emotional or otherwise), reach for the headphones.

classical emotional conditioning and emotional learning

We can learn to associate emotions with any object, person, or event. This learning is based on the classical conditioning paradigm commonly associated with Pavlov and his dogs.

Classical Conditioning

The Russian scientist Ivan Pavlov famously managed to condition his dogs to salivate not only at the prospect of food appearing (a normal, unlearned response), but at the mere sound of a bell. He did this by pairing the bell with the appearance of food; before long, the bell alone was enough to induce a salivation reaction in the dogs. The bell became a conditioned stimulus to the salivation process (the conditioned response).

Less well-known experiments by Pavlov show that if a bell is sounded before a dog is given a painful shock, the bell soon comes to elicit the same emotional responses associated with fear that are automatically elicited by the shock. This is referred to as negative emotional conditioning, because the dog learns to make the negative emotional responses to the bell as a result of conditioning.

It has been shown that humans, just like Pavlov's dogs, can learn to make positive or negative emotional responses to happy or unhappy events that occur in their lives. Conditioning theorists suggest that most of the likes and dislikes as well as the preferences and biases that make up our personality develop through emotional conditioning. This is because they are based on feelings that are aroused by positive and negative events. For example, if we encounter a stranger while simultaneously experiencing an unpleasant event, we feel more negative toward that stranger. Similarly, it is often said by chemotherapy patients that eating their favorite foods during treatment is likely to create a future aversion to those foods, as they associate the unpleasant feelings of treatment with that food.

Emotional Learning

Many children experience negative emotional conditioning at school that results in academic disengagement that affects their entire future. Perhaps they struggle with reading or math, or have a teacher who dislikes them. They may even have a hidden learning disability, such as dyslexia or attention deficit disorder, which causes them to be treated negatively by teachers and adults. The child learns to associate similar tasks (working with numbers, reading, and so on), or even school in general, with negative feelings. This negative emotional conditioning can result in inattention, truancy, lack of motivation, and ultimately, poor self-esteem and low educational achievement.

The effects of this can be minimized by replacing the negative conditioning with positive emotional conditioning experiences. Praising and giving rewards allows a child to associate positive feelings with learning and school, and can set the stage of high self-esteem and subsequent achievement.

Create Your Own Conditioning

Wouldn't it be great if you could stimulate a desired emotion in yourself at will? Well, using principles of emotional learning, you can invoke happiness, joy, excitement, or whatever emotion you want, whenever you want! Athletes can use this technique to feel confident before a match or race, as can presenters or speakers who would otherwise feel nervous before giving a lecture.

The trick is to find an "anchor"—something that you can use to associate an emotion with an event. For example, next time you are having a great day at the seaside with your kids, take the time to select a nice pebble or shell. Rub it, smell it, hold it throughout the day. You'll be feeling great because you're having a lovely day out—and you'll be learning to associate the great feeling of being carefree in the sun with that pebble. Now, take the pebble to work with you and put it in a drawer. (This is important; if you leave it constantly on show, you will simply habituate and the learned response will fade away, which is why holiday souvenirs soon lose their appeal when put on display back home.) Next time you feel stressed, dig out that pebble and stroke it, smell it, and so on. (Although it's perhaps best to do this out of sight of your colleagues!) Your mood should lift.

If you get really good at this, just thinking about the pebble, or conjuring up an image of it, should eventually be enough to lift your spirits.

the fallibility of forecasting

Affective forecasting means, quite simply, predicting how we will feel at some point in the future. It's about trying to imagine how an event will make us feel; something we can be surprisingly bad at. For example, most people believe that if they won the lottery then their happiness level would dramatically increase. In fact, researchers show that, a year or two on, most lottery winners are just as happy, or unhappy, as they always were.

Impact Bias

The reason that our affective forecasting skills are often poor is due to cognitive or mental biases that we're all vulnerable to. One of the most common biases is called the "impact bias." This is where we fail to appreciate the impact an event will have on our mood or happiness. For example, we believe that we'd be happy for many months if only our team were to win the cup. Or that we would never be happy again if our romantic relationship were to dissolve. In fact, most of these everyday events don't have as big an impact on our levels of happiness as we predict. But why is this?

One reason is that humans have a psychological defense system that allows us to cope with all kinds of adversity. We rationalize bad things that happen to us: My spouse has left me? Well, I'm better off without her really! We lost the championship? Well, we can only go up from here then! Life does go on, and we have mental processes to help us bounce back. The thing about affective forecasting is that we tend not to take these coping strategies into consideration when thinking about how an event is likely to impact on us.

We also fail to consider the human ability to adapt to both good and bad events. Our elation at winning the cup, getting promotion, or whatever the happy event is, only lasts so long—we quickly adapt to even the most pleasurable events. They quickly become just part of the background of daily life, which is why living the dream of emigrating to a holiday destination is never going to feel quite the same as the annual fortnight in the sun did.

Does it Matter?

Yes, it does indeed matter in some cases. Take, for example, the idea of "living wills"—in which healthy people specify that in the event of their ever being so ill that their quality of life reaches a certain low, they wish to refuse medical intervention. However, when it actually comes to such a point, researchers have shown that many people suffering even a very low quality of life, nevertheless want to live on. The problem of affective forecasting is that, until we're exposed to a particular reality, we just don't know how we'll feel about it.

How Good Is Your Affective Forecasting?

Which would make you happier:

- a job offering more money or better job security?
- a new car or a nice holiday?
- your child being top of the class or their winning a kindness award?
- going to a party or out for a meal with your partner?
- new clothes for you or for your kids?
- an act of kindness from a stranger or from your friend?

Author's Comments
These items are designed to help you think about your own affective forecasting ability; but, in truth, there's no surefire way of knowing how you'd feel about something until it happens—this is the moral of the affective forecasting story.

Miswanting

It was Daniel Gilbert, a professor of psychology at Harvard, who developed the idea of affective forecasting. And he has also coined the term "miswanting." He believes that the fallibility of affective forecasting means that we make poor decisions about what will make us happy—we "miswant." We think that the things we want—more money, a better car, a different relationship—will make us happy. Yet, getting what we think we want just leads us to want more, and we are no happier than when we started.

Acquiring new possessions, for example, only makes us happy for a short time; before long, we see something else that we "need" to make us happy. We're also happier with choices we make when other options are then closed to us; if we choose a certain product but then have the option of changing our minds, we're less happy than if our choice is irrevocable.

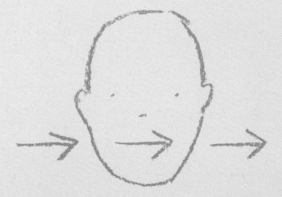

emotional intelligence

Emotional intelligence, popularized by Daniel Goleman in 1995, refers to the ability to identify, recognize, and manage our own emotions as well as those of others around us. According to this approach, conventional intelligence is too narrow a concept to be all-defining of success. Success requires more than a high IQ (from "Intelligence Quotient"), which has tended to be the traditional measure of intelligence. Most of us know people who are academically brilliant but socially inept. And we know that despite possessing a high IQ, success does not automatically follow. Emotional intelligence, then, is that aspect of intelligence that contributes to our social skill and awareness.

The EQ Model

In his book, *Emotional Intelligence: Why It Can Matter More Than IQ*, Goleman outlines his model of four main components of emotional intelligence:

1. Self-awareness: being aware of our own emotions and using this awareness to guide decisions.

2. Self-management: controlling and managing one's emotions.

3. Social awareness: the ability to sense, understand, and react to others' emotions.

4. Relationship management: the ability to inspire, influence, and develop others while managing conflict.

Goleman includes a set of emotional "competencies" within each of his four constructs of Emotional Quotient. Emotional competencies are not innate talents, but rather learned capabilities that must be worked on and developed in order to achieve outstanding performance. Goleman posits that individuals are born with a general emotional intelligence that determines their potential for learning emotional competencies. The construct "Emotional Quotient" is used as a measure of emotional intelligence.

What Is Your EQ?

How much do you agree with the following items?

- I'm usually aware of what my friends think of each other.
- When I'm upset, I usually know what's making me feel this way.
- People consider me to be a warm and approachable individual.
- I consider myself to be a good judge of character.
- I rely on my instincts when making a decision.
- I'm aware of my own skills and abilities.
- People tend to tell me their problems.
- If a co-worker is doing something that bothers me, I will tend to tell them.
- I'm usually good at knowing when someone is upset, even if they don't tell me.
- I'm considered a good peace-maker if there is a conflict.

Scale:

1 = strongly agree
2 = agree
3 = disagree
4 = strongly disagree

Can It Be Learned?

So, can this form of intelligence be learned, or is it rather static like general intelligence? The answer, it would seem, is a little of both. Just as it is thought that there is a genetic aspect to someone's Intelligence Quotient (IQ), so it is thought that there is a genetic aspect to someone's Emotional Quotient (EQ).

When a child is born, she or he will have an emotional potential that is determined by both genetic components and impacts made throughout their life—such as the influence of parents and other role-models. The combination of favorable genetic material and life influences will lead to an emotionally intelligent adult; however, if an individual has the potential but lacks a favorable environment to allow this to flourish, it is thought that training or learning can be beneficial later on. Even without a great genetic emotional potential, the right environment or training can maximize a person's emotional intelligence.

Developing Your EQ

1. Identify Your Emotions: Familiarize yourself with your body's response to excitement, joy, frustration, anger, disappointment, and so on. This will allow you to recognize your own feelings, anticipate them, and eventually learn to control them.

2. Listen to Your Feelings: Although being rational is very highly rated when it comes to decision-making, the emotionally intelligent individual should be aware of his or her "gut" feelings too. Imagine that you have chosen a particular course of action and identify how you would feel—relieved, disappointed perhaps? These gut feelings should not be ignored.

3. Be Aware: Try to understand the feelings that others are experiencing. Watch others' verbal and non-verbal language closely to see if you can "read" them accurately.

Score
The lower your score, the higher your EQ is likely to be. (Please note, this is a fun quiz and not a diagnostic tool!)

Chapter 4

love's emotions

what is love?

Views on love vary, but it's without doubt one of the most prevalent issues in our culture. Films, songs, and books all have love as their dominant theme, and advertisers clearly believe it to be a powerful seller. But books like this one sometimes seem intent on reducing love to a set of biochemical reactions, evolutionary hangovers, or unconscious urges. What if love just doesn't exist?

The Birth of Romantic Love?

Some scholars have suggested that what we think of in the West as "romantic love" is a cultural creation that emerged in France in the 11th century. Classically, this involved a knight seeing a beautiful but unattainable lady from afar, whose hand he would win by completing a quest. Replace the knight and lady with other characters and you have the plot for an infinite number of books, films, and songs.

So, is this where romantic love began or is it more universal than that? University of Nevada anthropologists conducted a study published in 1992 that explored whether "passionate sexual love" (apart from pure lust) existed in other cultures. They gathered evidence from 166 cultures around the globe, finding such things as love songs, experiences of longing and anguish, and elopement in almost 90 percent of the cultures. Although there are differences in the way love is expressed, the phenomenon seems to be universal.

Cultural reactions to romantic love, however, differ widely. The ancient Greeks believed that male and female were two sides of the same person, severed by Zeus, drawn to each other to become complete. Freud, on the other hand, described it as a "temporary psychosis." When psychologist James R. Averill asked for responses to a newspaper clipping about a couple who met, fell in love, and got engaged all on the same train journey, 40 percent of people said they could confirm the type of feeling involved, but the same proportion of

people had an unfavorable reaction. Perhaps some of us are just more romantic than others.

One Love or Many?

Helen Fisher from Rutgers University has identified three elements to the experience of love. First there is the lust phase, which is quite chemically driven and perhaps not very discriminating. Then there is romantic love, where the preference for a particular partner becomes overwhelming. Fisher explains that this drive is even stronger than hunger and, less romantically, notes how compulsive thoughts about a partner are similar to mania and obsessive-compulsive disorder. The final stage is long-term affection, a calmer, more comfortable, and more secure relationship with fewer emotional highs and lows. This may sound very familiar to you, and it makes a lot of evolutionary sense.

The idea is that as our evolutionary ancestors began to walk in an upright posture, the baby could no longer cling to the mother while she got on with what she needed to do. Pair bonding therefore developed so the male could take more of a role in supporting and protecting the infant during its long, vulnerable development. The male wanted to be sure the child was his and therefore required exclusivity, whereas the female wanted to be sure that the male would be around for long enough to provide support and resources. As such, the emotion of love, with its recognizable behaviors, could be a way of ensuring and checking on this relationship.

Victim of Love?

Much of the language we use in relation to love casts us as passive. We speak as if love happens to us, rather than as if we are instigators of it. We've variously "fallen in love," "been smitten," "lost our heart," and been "love-struck." Eros fires his little arrows while Shakespeare's Puck applies his lotion, and we're powerless to resist. There may be a little truth in this: it does seem that when we fall in love the parts of the neocortex that are involved in critical and negative thinking are suppressed. However, for the most part, we're far from powerless; and psychologists have found that simply recalling romantic moments with your partner is a good way of resisting the temptation to roam.

love's biochemistry

We all accept that chemicals can affect the way we feel and behave. Alcohol, cocaine, tobacco, and anti-depressants all change our mood and some can change our attitudes toward others. Nevertheless, we're resistant to the idea that love is a biochemical matter. It's just so unromantic. Yet research is steadily revealing the chemicals that help us love.

Love Drugs

Many people have heard of the hormones testosterone and estrogen, which affect sexual behavior. But there are many other chemicals at work in sexual relationships. The release of the neurotransmitter norepinephrine gives us that racing heart and feeling of excitement, whereas phenylalanine and dopamine make us feel good. In combination we have a heady cocktail of elation, excitement, energy, and craving. After sex, endogenous opiates (similar to heroin) flood our brains, making us feel cosy and relaxed.

This all sounds rather unromantic, but, if we truly have evolved according to the principle of survival of the fittest, it makes sense that we might enjoy and be rewarded for sex so that we create more offspring. It seems unquestionable that arousal and good feelings are related to chemicals, but what about affection and love? What about marriage?

Only 3 percent of mammals are monogamous, mating for life. Comparing these species with close relatives that are not monogamous can help us understand a great deal about love; surprisingly, voles have been particularly helpful here.

The Love Vole

Prairie voles might be seen as deeply romantic creatures. They mate for life, groom each other, and nest together, they make affectionate parents and the males get quite jealous and chase other males off. Montane voles, on the other hand, are more promiscuous and less exclusive in their mating habits.

One of the biggest differences between the two types of vole is the level of a hormone called oxytocin. Oxytocin is thought to be involved in maternal behaviors such as lactation and bonding with infants, but it's also released during sex and is thought to bond the partners together and make social interaction and affection more rewarding. Increasing the level of oxytocin in prairie voles makes them more sociable and less aggressive; interestingly, it also increases their preference for sticking with one partner. They don't even need to mate for this preference to emerge.

Will it Work for You?

Humans also have oxytocin and it does seem to be related to loving behavior, though there has been much less research on how it works for us. However, we do know that oxytocin levels increase when women talk about intense feelings of warmth for other people. Research has also shown that, after an administration of oxytocin, people become more altruistic and a lot more generous when playing games against other people—though not when playing against computers. It seems that one of the main effects of the hormone is to help people see things from others' perspectives. However, it doesn't appear to be a wonder drug to make people fall in love.

A Fidelity Drug?

So can we make our promiscuous montane voles act more like loving prairie voles? A simple injection doesn't appear to do the trick, as it's the number of receptors that seems to be critical. Prairie voles' brains have many more receptors that are stimulated by oxytocin, so even if you increase the amount of oxytocin in montane voles they can't use it. However, there is another hormone, vasopressin, which seems to have similar effects. Larry Young and his team at the Young Lab in Atlanta found that if they increased the number of vasopressin receptors genetically, the montane vole does appear to act more like a prairie vole.

Is That it, Then?

It may seem a little depressing to have love, one of the most important of human emotions, reduced to a matter of mere hormones and receptors, but that's clearly far from the whole picture. To say that you fell in love with someone because of the amount of oxytocin released into your brain may be like saying you didn't run someone over in your car because of the brake fluid being pumped toward the brakes. The hormone doesn't adequately describe the reasoning and volition behind it. We're not indiscriminate love machines driven to fall in love by a chemical being squirted at the right (or wrong!) time, despite occasional appearances to the contrary.

attachment theory

A lot of psychology sounds much like common sense. In this section you'll hear that infants often have a special bond with caregivers such as their mothers, and that they get anxious when this person is not around. You probably didn't need a psychologist to tell you that, but psychology can help us understand why and how these things happen, and what the implications are.

Imprinting

Sometimes the key to getting a family is just being in the right place at the right time. Specifically, if you want a family of geese then you need to be there on day one of their lives. It seems that goslings of this age will select the most plausible moving and noise-making object as their mother and follow it. Once the bond is made, it's highly persistent.

Zoologist Konrad Lorenz dubbed this process "imprinting." He suggests that we are preprogrammed to carry out certain behaviors that are triggered by a "releaser" as soon as we've reached the right stage of our development. In the example above, upon hatching the goslings have reached the point where they are ready to bond to a mother. They have some basic criteria for identifying what a mother is (something that moves and makes a noise), so acquiring a family of geese is simply a matter of making sure you're the "releaser" who meets those criteria.

Attachment Theory

British psychiatrist John Bowlby was influenced by Lorenz's ideas as he developed his "attachment theory." According to this theory, infants are driven, at a specific developmental point, to bond very closely with one or more caregivers, such as parents. When these caregivers are nearby the children feel secure enough to explore their environment; they are the best able to calm and comfort their children and are the ones children will seek for play or security. The relationship is most evident in novel or frightening situations.

It's not clear who takes the lead in forming the relationship, though it seems to be reciprocal between the child and the adult. However, Bowlby suggests that the infant uses a range of behaviors such as crying, cooing, clinging, and smiling to attract the adult. He saw this as the same kind of process as imprinting, and as a routine that infants have to ensure their safety by bonding a trusted person to them.

Bowlby felt that these attached relationships, when warm, continuous, and intimate, were essential to mental health and successful future relationships. Experiments with monkeys showed that those deprived of attachment with a caregiver became dysfunctional adults and performed poorly both socially and intellectually.

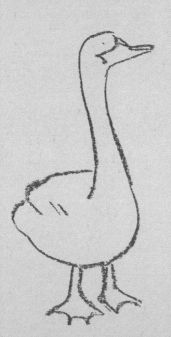

Separation Anxiety

The price of being close to someone is that you miss them when they're gone. Starting between 7 and 12 months of age, children generally become very distressed when the person to whom they're attached leaves.

This anxiety has a remarkably consistent pattern around the world, peaking at 15 to 18 months then gradually reducing until about the age of three, as the child learns to appreciate that the caregiver will return. This applies regardless of whether the adult spends a lot of time with the child and whether they are particularly warm. Those without attachments, such as those brought up in some institutions, don't suffer in this way.

The Strange Situation

Mary Ainsworth, a close colleague of Bowlby's, designed a method of measuring attachment called "the strange situation." The adult, the child, and a stranger spend set amounts of time together and the reactions of the child are noted when the adult leaves and then returns.

"Securely attached" children, around 65 percent of Americans, go to the adult and accept comfort from them when they return. Around 20 percent were "resistant"; distressed at the leaving and alternately clinging to and resisting the adult when they returned. The remaining "avoidant" 15 percent ignored both the leaving and the return.

However, these responses reflect cultural values. German culture puts more emphasis on children being independent, and many more German children were "avoidant." In traditional Japanese families (but not in untraditional ones), where children are rarely left with anyone but the primary caregiver, no children were "avoidant" and many more were "resistant."

the secrets of attraction

Beauty is in the eye of the beholder, tastes differ, and fashion impacts on who and what we find attractive. True. But it's not the whole story.

It seems that there is fairly universal agreement on some aspects of what makes a person attractive. Even if they're not to your taste, most would agree that Marilyn Monroe, George Clooney, and Claudia Schiffer are physically attractive people. Even two-month-old babies will spend longer looking at a face that raters have agreed is attractive than at a less attractive face.

Attraction from Evolution

Although preferences for hairstyle, weight, and the like may change with the times, people almost invariably rate symmetrical faces and bodies as being more attractive. This makes evolutionary sense, as symmetry is a good indicator of health, genetic fitness, and also damage sustained in the womb.

We also tend to prefer "average" faces. If a number of photographs are combined ("morphed") to create an average, the more photos that are included, the more attractive the end result tends to be. This attraction to the average, called *koinophilia*, again makes evolutionary

sense; extreme faces with unusually placed or sized features may signal pathology, making the average face a safe bet.

The finding that males list youth as a priority when choosing a mate, whereas females give higher ratings to wealth, ambition, and prestige, also supports evolutionary theory. In primitive societies a young wife will likely have greater child-bearing potential, whereas a more successful man is likely to be better able to support the child.

The Attraction of Masculinity

Particularly masculine features such as heavy brows and broader chins are the result of higher levels of testosterone and are often associated with competitiveness and thrill-seeking behaviors. In evolutionary terms those who display such features should be good hunters but less likely to engage in long-term relationships and child nurturing.

Psychologist David Perrett, who heads the Perception

Lab at the University of St. Andrews, Scotland, has worked extensively with morphing technology to create several versions of the same photographic portrait. Some have more masculine features and others more feminine ones. Curiously, both men and women tend to prefer the more feminine faces, perhaps because they seem less threatening. However, other research found that those women who prefer the more masculine faces are also the ones most likely to be in uncommitted and short-term relationships. The exception is that when women are ovulating, their preference turns toward more masculine faces.

Women also tend to rate bravery very highly in a partner. In fact, this is a better predictor than kindness of whom women would choose as a long-term or short-term partner. It's also a better predictor of whom they would choose as a male friend. Surprisingly, when choosing someone for a short-term relationship, brave but unkind rated higher than brave and kind as a combination!

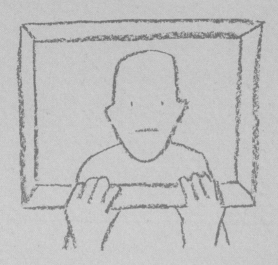

Looks or Brains?

When asked to rate the IQ of someone based purely on their photo, higher IQs are attributed to more physically attractive people. Psychologists have found that this may actually reflect reality and that beautiful people are, on average, smarter. This shouldn't really be surprising. If men are seeking the most beautiful women and women are seeking the men with the best prospects, then some people's offspring are likely to be more attractive and clever than other peoples'. It may not seem fair, but natural selection isn't—attractive people even get paid more. Using a five-point attractiveness scale, on average a man will earn U.S.$2,600 more than someone who is one point less attractive than him. When it comes to women, each point is worth an additional U.S.$2,150 to their salary.

You're So Vain

Ask a friend to make a snap decision on which of two reference numbers he or she prefers. Each should consist of three letters, four numbers, then a letter. However, the first three letters of one should relate to your friend's name; for example, its first three letters. People will tend to unconsciously choose the reference that is similar to their name.

This effect has been found quite consistently, and is even claimed to affect choices about careers and where to live. For example, Dennis may find dentistry appealing and Nessa nursing. This "implicit egotism" appears to be based on the comfort we find in familiar things. As dating can be quite stressful, similarities become reassuring and attractive. This could explain the finding that people favor partners who look a little like one of their parents, and Perrett's team has found that the face people find most attractive is actually a photo of themselves, morphed to look like the opposite sex.

sigmund freud

I once heard how a colleague, discussing the merits of several job applicants, said of a particularly good-looking one, "I am sure he would be a good bed." She protested that she had meant to say, "a good bet," but we were all confident that she had said what she meant, even if she hadn't meant to say it.

Such slips of the tongue are called "Freudian slips," named after the Austrian psychologist and neurologist Sigmund Freud (1856–1939). It was he, more than anyone, who gave us this idea that bubbling under our conscious mind there is an ocean of hidden memories, desires, and experiences that impact on our thoughts, feelings, and behavior. Although much of Freud's thinking is now widely rejected, it's hard to overestimate his impact on the way we all think about ourselves.

The Freudian Personality

For Freud there were three main elements to the personality. The "id" is the original inner mind, all desires and instincts. It constantly seeks to reduce the tension caused by stimuli such as hunger, thirst, or sexual desire, but is hampered by its inability to interact with the real world. If it's hungry it can't tell the difference between cheese and a memory or picture of cheese, so it can't satisfy its hunger. The second part, the "ego," develops to interact with the real world, to search out something that will more effectively satisfy our needs and restrain the id's impulse to satisfy them immediately with whatever comes to mind. The "super-ego" develops later as the rules and values of parents and society are internalized; it's our conscience and the ideals we want to live up to. Trying to balance and control the needs of the id and the demands of the super-ego while interacting with the external world is very demanding for the ego. Occasionally there will be thoughts, experiences, and desires that bring it into conflict with reality or with the super-ego, so "defense mechanisms" exist to protect the conscious mind from them. The most well-known of these mechanisms is "repression." This is where the thoughts and feelings are hidden away in the unconscious and forgotten. The problem is that they often refuse to lie down and be completely erased. They push their way through to conscious awareness, albeit usually in disguise. So it is that we make Freudian slips, our dreams fill with bizarre, inexplicable images, and we develop fears or affections for reasons we don't understand.

reud on Love and Sex

eud believed that the sexual
rive was fundamental to
e and the source of the id's
nergy.

the process of sexual
evelopment, the unrestrained
develops many thoughts
at are condemned by the
uper-ego and rejected by
e ego. These desires, which
ill never be acted upon,
rovoke anxiety within the
onscious mind, so they are
ften repressed. However,
epression is not the only
efense mechanism that
e mind has in its arsenal.
Displacement'' is where
is neither possible nor
ppropriate to direct your
eelings toward their true

target so you direct them
toward another. For example,
you may want to kiss your
boss but you can't, so you
pursue a colleague instead.
This creates a potentially
confusing romantic world
where you can never be sure
that you are truly attracted to
the person to whom you think
you are.

"Sublimation," a particular
form of displacement, is
where the sexual energy that
cannot be expressed because
of society's constraints is
redirected into creative
and cultural activities. For
Freud, much that is of value
in civilization is the result of
sublimated sexual energy.

The Oedipus Complex

he Oedipus complex
s probably the most
ontroversial aspect of
reud's thinking, but he
aw it as fundamental to his
nderstanding of personality.
he theory states that children
jo through a phase of being
erotically attracted to their
parent of the opposite sex,
nd feeling resentment and

hostility toward the same-sex
parent. Eventually the feelings
for the opposite-sex parent
turn to normal affection and
they internalize society's
taboos against incest.

For males, the mother is
now a de-eroticized figure.
Freud believed that if a man
feels warmth and tenderness

("love") toward a woman it
may well be because she
reminds him of his mother.
For that very reason, the
woman he has these feelings
for is unlikely to be the one
he feels sexual desire for. For
Freud, resolving this split was
critical to achieving good
romantic relationships.

making love last

You fall in love, settle down, then live happily ever after. For many this is the ideal storyline, but it doesn't always happen that way. Every year in Western countries between 1 and 5 percent of marriages are ended in divorce.

Even for those that stay together, there may not be a happy ending. Denise Previti and Paul Amato at Pennsylvania State University's Department of Sociology found that one quarter of married couples stay together only because they don't see a better alternative. This is often because separation is financially difficult or because their values, often religious ones, make them reluctant to divorce. Inevitably, many stay together to try and protect their children.

The Four Horsemen of the Apocalypse
Unsurprisingly, the main determinant of whether couples stay together seems to be the attitude that they have to each other. Psychologist John Gottman has conducted extensive research into break-ups and claims that spending just 15 minutes with a couple is enough to tell whether they will be together in a few years' time. His team has identified four behaviors that are the most damaging to marriage, which he has called the "four horseman of the apocalypse."

Couples are asked to discuss an area of conflict for 15 minutes. This reveals the presence or absence of the "horsemen."

1. Criticism: Discussions are typically started by the woman, and if she focuses on a general criticism of her partner rather than a particular incident, then the first horseman has arrived. For example, she might say "You never do anything to help in the kitchen," rather than "You just didn't bother to help that evening."

2. Defensiveness: It's normally the man responding, and if he becomes defensive rather than being open to what she is saying, this does not bode well.

3. Stonewalling: It's not uncommon for the man in particular to withdraw from the discussion or refuse to engage. Again, not a good sign.

4. Contempt: When the discussion is finished the couple discuss something more positive. If one of them (typically the man) continues to display contempt towards the other we have the fourth horseman, and this appears to be the worst of all.

Gottman says that the first three minutes are often very revealing; the ratio of positive to negative emotions being expressed is critical.

Using just this discussion, Gottman has been able to predict with 90 percent accuracy which couples will be together a few years down the road.

Love Is Blind

So what sets couples that stay together apart from those who don't? It shouldn't be a surprise that they are likely to think highly of each other, but the research suggests that this is often to an unrealistic degree.

Professor Sandra Murray, of the University at Buffalo, found that, in the United States, partners tend to rate each other as more similar to each other than they actually are. Further, wives (for example) rate their husband more highly than he rates himself, but also more highly than his friends rate him. Maybe that is how it should be; I should think more highly of my wife than other people do, as I am the one who chose to marry her and who wants to live with her.

Norm O'Rourke and Philippe Cappeliez call this "marital aggrandizement" and have found that those in longer-term relationships rate their partners as nicer than they actually are. These "Pollyannas" believe themselves to be living in the best of marital worlds.

Generational Differences

One of the difficulties in establishing what makes relationships last is that those who have been together a long time are usually of a different generation to those just starting out in their relationships. However, one of the big differences that psychologists have noticed is that older couples don't tend to take so much notice of negative things that a partner says about them. Paul Zeitlow and Allan Sillars have noted that they are less likely to explore and open up their feelings in depth than younger couples are. As a result there are fewer points of major disagreement.

Keeping it Exciting

It might seem a cliché, but Art Aron at Stony Brook University, New York, has found evidence to back up the received wisdom that boredom is one of the key threats to relationships. Spending time together is important, but doing the same things all the time may not be ideal. Doing something exciting or even just something new can trigger the release of dopamine, which could reinforce positive feelings about the relationship.

the jealous heart

"O! Beware, my lord, of jealousy; it is the green-eyed monster which doth mock the meat it feeds on." Iago, from Shakespeare's *Othello*

Othello, the eponymous "Moor of Venice" in Shakespeare's play, is the archetypical victim of jealousy: deeply in love with his wife yet tormented by jealous thoughts that eventually drive him to kill her. However, some psychologists suggest that jealousy is not an entirely negative emotion.

Helpful Jealousy

From an evolutionary perspective, jealousy is taken to have evolved from a need to preserve the pair-bond relationship from external threats. It may be the inevitable result of the monogamous relationships that have been the social norm throughout history. (Although the practice of polygamy is a notable exception, and has occurred in many cultures, it's relatively unusual and often the preserve of the rich and powerful.) Jealousy alerts partners to threats to the relationship but is also a sign of commitment. Even today, if you don't feel jealous when your partner shows a lot of interest in someone else it may cause your commitment and love for them to be called into question.

Jealousy could, therefore, be seen as an appropriate response to a relationship under threat. This even stretches to the sphere of religion; where, for example, the Abrahamic religions (Judaism, Christianity, and Islam) describe their God as jealous. There are warnings against the worship of "false gods," and the relationship between God and the Church is often presented as a marriage.

Jealousy is not restricted to romantic relationships and it's often noted how jealous a child can be if a sibling or parent pays too much attention to someone else. However, romantic jealousy is a particularly dangerous emotion as it's aroused when what we value most is threatened: our love, trust, role, family, and self-esteem. Research by Susanne Dell in 1984 revealed that 17 percent of homicides in the United Kingdom were related to "amorous jealousy and possessiveness."

Morbid Jealousy

When jealousy becomes extreme it's referred to as "morbid jealousy," of which there are two main strands. The first, "obsessive jealousy," is the situation in which a person can't get rid of the idea that a partner is being unfaithful even when, thinking rationally, this can't be the case. With "psychotic jealousy" the person truly believes that a partner is unfaithful; testing and checking for it, with the potential to become violent. It is often a facet of other conditions such as paranoid schizophrenia, brain damage, or drug and alcohol abuse.

Jealousy vs. Envy

These two emotions are easily confused, but psychologists Laura Guerrero and Peter Anderson point out that jealousy relates to loss, specifically the fear, sadness, and anger of losing a loved one to someone else. Envy is related to something you don't have but somebody else does. Jealousy says, "It's mine, don't take it away"; envy says, "It's yours and I want it."

Morbid jealousy can be particularly worrying because of the risk of violence. In the mid-1960s Horace B. Mooney reported that 14 percent of morbidly jealous males in the United Kingdom had made homicidal attempts and 20 percent had attempted suicide.

Different cultures seem to have broadly the same expressions of jealousy, though males and females do differ in the ways they respond. Psychiatrists Geoffrey White and Paul Mullen have researched jealousy extensively and they report a tendency for jealous women to be more attentive to their partners and try to appease them. Men, on the other hand, are likely to seek solace and retribution elsewhere, possibly by having an affair.

The Jealous Sort

Try this brief questionnaire.

1. Do you feel uncomfortable when your partner flirts with someone else?

2. Would you be at all troubled if your partner kept secrets from you about who they were spending their time with?

3. Do you think it's wrong to flirt with other people in front of your partner?

4. Would you be at all troubled if your partner chose to spend a lot of time with someone that you knew they found attractive?

Author's Comments

If you replied "no" to most of these, you may not be a very jealous person, but you may also be the type of person who makes your partner jealous. Your partner might well ask how committed you are if you think all of this is OK!

gaining your affection

Have you ever tried to throw a teddy bear away? Some of us find it very difficult. The rational part of the mind tells us the bear is made of fluff and fur, but nevertheless we can't help noticing the particularly sad look on its face making us feel guilty, as if we're abandoning it.

Anthropomorphism

Humans readily ascribe human thoughts and feelings to objects that don't have them. This "anthropomorphism" is one of the reasons we find it so hard to evaluate whether animals can truly think and feel—if we worry about a teddy bear's feelings then we may not be very rational and objective when deciding whether a real puppy can experience sadness.

Cuddly toys are designed to elicit emotions from us, but even machines and anonymous organizations can do it. A business's ability to get our money often depends on it. It's called "brand loyalty," but the emotion often runs deeper than this suggests and can be closer to affection. For example, when choosing a new car, fridge, or can of baked beans you may weigh up a number of factors in making your decision, but often you're simply gathering information to support the decision you want to make.

Affection and Familiarity

In some ways our loyalty and affection can be very easily bought and without our knowledge. The Polish-born social psychologist Robert Zajonc showed how even the slightest exposure to something can affect the way we feel, and that familiarity with something develops a preference for it. This may sound obvious—we know that if you advertise and get your brand name known then people are more likely to buy your product—but Zajonc showed that the effect can be far more subtle than that.

One example involves subjects being shown two Chinese ideograms and asked which they prefer. People generally favor the one they have seen before. They don't need to have seen it for very long at all. In fact, even if people are shown the image for such a short time that they do not consciously register what they saw, the effect persists.

It seems that we evaluate something emotionally before making a conscious decision about it, and that brief emotional response is enough to make us prefer it. Zajonc calls this the "mere exposure" effect, and the amazing thing is that the less aware of the first image we are, the stronger our preference seems to be.

Happy Products

A great way of influencing feelings is to give a quick cue as to what you want someone to feel. Zajonc conducted another experiment in which people were again shown some Chinese ideograms. But before they saw each one they were shown a face that was either smiling or frowning. It was shown for only 1/200th of a second and then followed immediately by another image to ensure that the mind didn't focus on the face. People were unaware of having seen the face but still they preferred the ideograms that had been preceded by the smiling face to those preceded by a frown.

That's not to say you can make someone like something purely by flashing them a quick image—but it can influence their decision. Another study showed how, in a dispute between two strangers, people will more often side with the one whose face they briefly and unconsciously saw prior to meeting.

Love the One You're With

People can get bored and look for novelty, believing that "The grass is greener on the other side." However, research also shows that once we have made a decision, whether choosing a partner, a car, or a holiday, our commitment to it normally grows. In one piece of research, women were shown a range of products and asked to rate them for how attractive they were. Two products that had been rated equally attractive were then offered to the person who had done the rating and she was told she could have one of them. After she had made her choice, she was asked to rate them all again. The one she had chosen was rated higher than before, the one she rejected was rated lower than before. So it is with brands. Once you have bought into a particular car brand, assuming that nothing awful happens, you have made some level of emotional commitment to that brand.

Chapter 5

the angers

the anger response

Like most human emotions, anger is usually a healthy part of our emotional repertoire. When we feel angry, it's the body's way of signaling that something is wrong, that we're not happy, and that we need to take action.

Historically, our ancestors' anger would have alerted them to the fact that, for example, a rival was stealing food or prized possessions; the strong feelings generated by the emotion would have stimulated the victim to fight for his rights and his possessions. The emotional response would have created physiological changes in the body (more on this later) which would produce extra strength, resources, and energy to fight. Without that strength of feeling, our cave-dwelling ancestors would have been too laid-back to be bothered with aggressors or rivals—and wouldn't have survived long.

Today, the causes of our anger may be different, but the strength of feeling is still just as powerful in many people. If, for example, we're being taken advantage of at work, anger motivates us to take action. Anger, then, can be a very important emotion, despite the bad press that it receives; it motivates us to take action against perceived unfairness, it signals to us that a wrong has been committed, and it draws attention (both ours and others') to problems that need to be addressed. The problem is that we're rarely able to deal with our anger by the physical means available to our less civilized ancestors; today, dealing with anger is far more complex and has to obey the "rules of engagement" of the society we live in.

The Angry Personality
Many people ask if there is such a thing as an "angry personality." There are indeed people who are more "threat-sensitive" than others; their personalities and genetic make-up, as well as learned experiences throughout

their lives, make them more likely to produce the anger response without needing much provocation. The good news is that this trait can be changed, and angry people can become a lot calmer in general.

There is a range of factors that can contribute to an "angry" personality; these can be divided into cognitive and affective factors.

Cognitive Factors

These mental processes include our interpretation of events and our expectations of them. Events are only anger-eliciting if we appraise them or interpret them to be so. This is why the same events can occur to the same people but only some of us will interpret them in ways that make us feel angry. We talk of people taking things "too personally"; or in psychological terms, of being too "threat-sensitive."

When our expectations are very high, we can end up irritated and frustrated, which can lead to anger. We expect things to be perfect, to go well, or for others to reach our high standards, and when they don't, we get angry.

Affective Factors

Feelings (or affective factors) also contribute to how angry a person is. People who are generally more tense, anxious, or stressed are more easily provoked. When we are tense, it does not take much to "send us over the edge." Minor setbacks are seen as catastrophes and small irritations become major grievances.

Linked to tension is the issue of becoming too serious about things, and being unable to distance ourselves enough to put things in perspective. We may find that we don't laugh as much as we used to, or seem to have lost our sense of humor. Things that we might once have laughed at or shrugged off make us angry instead.

frustration and aggression

Most of us know what anger is, but it's easy to confuse with aggression and frustration. It's useful to separate these terms to help understand them and their relationship to anger.

Frustration is often a precursor to anger; it's the feeling we experience when we don't get what we want, when obstacles are put in our way, or when someone interferes with our attempts to achieve goals. At work, telephone interruptions, colleagues popping by for a chat, the computer server being slow, the photocopier breaking down—all these are the sorts of frustrations that can easily build to create workplace anger.

Aggression, on the other hand, is the action that can result from the feeling of being angry. It's usually intended to cause physical or emotional harm to others, perhaps with verbal insults, threats, sarcasm, or raised voices. When aggression becomes so extreme that we lose self-control, it's said that we are in a rage. Such a person is characterized as being very loud—shouting or screaming—going red in the face, shaking, threatening, and perhaps even becoming violent.

Frustration–Aggression

According to the frustration–aggression hypothesis, (put forward by John Dollard and Neal Miller in 1939), when people think that they are being prevented from achieving a goal, their frustration is likely to turn to aggression. The closer they get to reaching that goal, the greater the excitement and expectation of achievement will be. Thus the closer they are, the more frustrated they will get by being held back—and the more likely they will be to exhibit some form of aggressive behavior. Unexpected occurrence of the frustration also increases the likelihood of aggression.

If the source of the frustration cannot easily be targeted for aggression—for example, your boss might be too powerful, or an online store that has let you down might be inaccessible—your aggression might be directed elsewhere. The victim is a scapegoat, or someone you consider an "outsider" to your own circle.

All this helps explain how aggression can escalate at sports matches.

Types of Aggression

Aggression can be instrumental, whereby no harm is in itself intended—it's just a means (instrument) to another goal. For example, toddlers trying to obtain a toy may shove other children out of the way, but their goal is to reach the toy, not to cause harm deliberately.

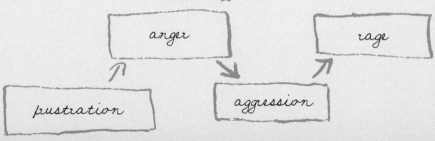

Aggression can also be either antisocial or prosocial. Antisocial aggression intends harm in terms of a violation of socially acceptable norms; for example, a thug mugging you for your wallet is committing antisocial aggression. On the other hand, prosocial aggression is that which takes place for the good of society; for example, a police officer apprehending the thug by using physical force is using prosocial aggression.

Aggression and the Media
In 1982 the U.S. National Institute of Mental Health published a ten-year study of the effects of watching television. Its conclusion was that about 80 percent of all programs in the United States contain violence, with an average of 5.2 violent acts per hour. The rates were highest during the day and on weekends, when children are often the viewers.

Canadian psychologist Albert Bandura performed early research in 1963 in the form of the now-classic "Bobo" doll studies. These looked at young children's imitation of novel acts of aggressive behavior (aggressive acts the children were unlikely to perform spontaneously) that they witnessed adults performing. The results showed that those exposed to examples of aggression were indeed more likely to act aggressively themselves, which suggests that we might learn aggression by watching it on television.

In 1974 Leonard Berkowitz investigated the television-watching habits of a group of boys when they were nine years old and then returned ten years later to study their levels of aggression. The results were consistent with Bandura's findings: those who had watched the most violence on television as children were the most aggressive aged 19.

Violent Witness

For the next week, keep a record of every violent act you witness in any media form. You can do this either with a list of ticks (a tick for every violent image seen), or a more sophisticated form whereby acts are classified into instrumental, antisocial, and prosocial types. Monitor your television viewing, newspaper images, adverts, cinema, computer games, and so on. You may be shocked at how much violence you routinely accept as part of everyday life. Is this damaging? Are you desensitized to certain types of violence? Do you feel more angry or aggressive after viewing violent images?

Yet more evidence of a link was found by David P. Phillips, of the University of California, when in 1983 he published findings that the number of murders in the United States significantly increased after boxing matches were aired on television.

daily hassles and life stressors

Anger tends to be exacerbated both by the accumulation of minor "daily hassles" and by the bigger, more stressful life events or "life stressors." Sometimes, the minor hassles can be the "straw that broke the camel's back" and send us over the edge in terms of our anger response. Often, it's these daily hassles against a backdrop of major life events that can tip the balance for us.

Daily Hassles

The daily irritants that we all encounter on a daily basis include events such as running out of milk for our morning coffee, missing the bus, being late for work, the computer crashing, losing a document, and so on. These tend to fall into such categories as, for example, "interruptions," "thwarted goals," and "time pressures." It's the accumulation of these little things that can really add to our daily stress— and those of us with higher stress levels tend to be more likely to fly off the handle. This is the drip-drip effect.

Berkeley-based psychologist Allen Kanner developed a questionnaire to measure the daily hassles that each of us comes across that cause us stress. In 1981 his research showed that the six top daily hassles were:

• concerns about weight
• the health of a family member
• the rising price of common goods
• home maintenance.
• having too many things to do
• misplacing or losing things.

It's often the daily hassles that cause us to lose our temper rather than more serious life events. How often have we lost it when we are interrupted for the fifth time that morning by our colleagues, subordinates, or kids asking a stupid question? Or how angry and frustrated do we feel when we are under pressure to submit a report but the computer isn't responding? How irrationally angry do we get when someone cuts in front of us in the supermarket queue (so-called "shopping-cart rage") or in the slow-moving traffic jam ("road rage")? All these angry episodes are the results of an accumulation of daily stressors, not the major life events.

Life Stressors

Research in 1967 by psychiatrists Thomas Holmes and Richard Rahe has revealed a list of "life stressors"—major life events that are stressful. They used this list to develop the "Holmes and Rahe social readjustment scale." The scale is a list of the main life stressors (not all of which are negative events), each of which is given a number of points: the most stressful on the list is death of a spouse and the least stressful is a minor violation of the law. The research indicates that if your total score is more than 150 points the chances are that it could have an impact on your health. A score of over 300 points in one year indicates that you have a high risk of developing a stress-related health problem.

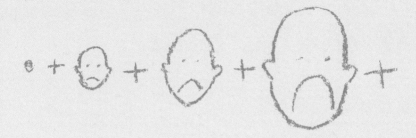

The Holmes and Rahe Social Readjustment Scale

Which of the following life events have happened to you in the past 12 months? Add up the points of all those that apply.

Death of a spouse	100	Trouble with in-laws	29
Divorce	73	Outstanding personal achievement	28
Marital separation	65	Spouse starts or stops work	26
Imprisonment	63	Begin or end school	26
Death of a close family member	63	Change in living conditions	25
Personal injury or illness	53	Revision of personal habits	24
Marriage	50	Trouble with boss	23
Dismissal from work	47	Change in working hours or	
Marital reconciliation	45	conditions	20
Retirement	45	Change in residence	20
Change in health of family member	44	Change in schools	20
Pregnancy	40	Change in recreation	19
Sexual difficulties	39	Change in church activities	19
Gain a new family member	39	Change in social activities	18
Business readjustment	39	Minor mortgage or loan	17
Change in financial state	38	Change in sleeping habits	16
Change in frequency of arguments	35	Change in number of family reunions	15
Major mortgage	32	Change in eating habits	15
Foreclosure of mortgage or loan	30	Vacation	13
Change in responsibilities at work	29	Christmas	12
Child leaving home	29	Minor violation of law	11

Scores

300 or more: At risk of illness.

150 to 299: Risk of illness is moderate (reduced by 30 percent from the above risk).

150 or below: Only have a slight risk of illness.

temper tantrums and the terrible twos

Babies are not born angry. They cry and scream in order to get what they want (and need), but the peak age for fully developed temper tantrums is around two—hence the "terrible twos." By this age, children know what it is to be angry—and so do their parents. They know that there are options and choices out there, but don't yet understand that they can't have whatever they want.

Tantrum Triggers

Most temper tantrums are triggered by a finite range of sources (though they may appear in various guises):

- Frustration at having goals thwarted—children want something, their parents say "no," so a tantrum ensues.
- Desire for independence—they want to walk, get out of their stroller, or get dressed themselves but their parents are short on the time required for such efforts.
- Inability to achieve desired effect (frustrated by their own limitations)—the puzzle pieces won't slot in, the t-shirt won't pull down, the seesaw won't "see" (or "saw"); any number of things can prove obstacles and triggers for those tantrums.

The common thread for all these themes is really wanting something that they can't have. Young children do not yet have the emotional control to reign in the strong feelings that this denial unleashes—nor do they have the cognitive capacities to put their disappointment into perspective. This is why they howl as much at a refusal of demands for small, transitory items such as chocolate as at the denial of longer-lasting goods such as expensive toys. All of this is a normal part of child development.

What Should Parents Do?

The response of many parents to their toddler's tantrum is either to get angry themselves or to give in to the child's demands. Getting angry is an understandable

Is a Child's Anger a Problem?

Does your toddler:

- Regularly bite other people when angry?
- Hurt people other than family members when angry; for example, nursery staff or other children?
- Fly into an uncontrollable rage at the slightest provocation?
- Hurt himself when angry; for example, by head-banging?
- Stay angry for a long time?

Author's Comments

If you answer "yes," to three or more of these, then you may need to get support. However, even a "yes," to all the items does not mean that your child will grow up with behavioral problems. All of the above are frequent behaviors at the age of two; but they are hard to deal with and expert input may help you to cope.

reaction, especially if the tantrum happens in public and the parent is embarrassed. Parents get angry because:

- They feel that the child is deliberately winding them up.
- They feel unable to control the situation.
- They themselves are thwarted in trying to achieve their own goals (getting the tantrum to stop and their child to co-operate).

However, getting angry, shouting, and losing their own temper is unlikely to solve the problem either in the short or long term. In fact, it teaches the child that anger outbursts are acceptable. It's better to act calmly (even if this is only an act) and ignore the behavior—however embarrassing it may be.

Heading Off a Tantrum
Parents can reduce the likelihood of a tantrum occurring by planning ahead:

- They should avoid letting their child become too tired or hungry; both can lead to irritability and anger outbursts (as they can in adults).
- Parents should ensure that their child is getting enough attention where possible. Tantrums often happen when parents have turned their attention elsewhere; for example, at the supermarket, while chatting to friends, and so on.
- It can be useful to try to distract a child who is ready to tantrum; this can be effective in the early stages.
- Parents should pick their battles and try to avoid saying "no" too much; too many "no"s can be very frustrating. For example, if a child asks for sweets, offer an alternative rather than just saying "no."

More Serious Problems
As most toddlers have frequent tantrums throughout the day, it's hard to identify anything that might indicate abnormalities at this stage. For example, a child with attention deficit hyperactivity disorder at age two is very hard to distinguish from a child who doesn't have this condition. Many angry toddlers grow into perfectly reasonable children once they are able to communicate and control their emotions better.

anger and health

Anger, like stress and other powerful emotions, has a profound effect on the body. As our anger rises, the hypothalamus in the brain stimulates the pituitary glands to release a range of hormones that affect every part of our body in one way or another. The main players are adrenaline and cortisol, and these exert their influence via the cardiovascular system and other organs. Adrenaline causes the heart to beat faster and blood pressure to rise; this allows oxygenated blood to flow to areas of the body that are responsible for reacting to the source of anger. Traditionally, the areas needing the extra energy would be the limbs (to run or fight) and the brain (to think faster), while blood is diverted from other less important areas such as the stomach. Extra energy is also provided by the release into the blood of extra sugar (glucose).

How Hostile Are You?

You may have a "hostile heart" if you:

- are intolerant of other people's mistakes
- are always suspicious of other people's motives
- often have strong negative feelings toward other people
- tend to be preoccupied with all that is wrong in your world
- frequently complain about what other people have done or said
- are always keen to point out other people's mistakes
- lose your temper easily
- rarely forget or forgive someone who has wronged you.

Anger and Health
The net effect of all this hormonal activity is a rapid heartbeat, breathlessness (as the lungs struggle to take in more oxygen), high blood pressure, and a raised body temperature (due to increasing energy expenditure). All this made our angry ancestors ideally placed to deal with the source of their anger as they used up new reserves of energy to, for example, fight rivals for scarce food resources.

These days, the physiological effects of anger are less useful. Rarely do we have the chance to respond to the source of our anger in the way that our bodily reactions have prepared us to. Rather than turn to aggression we're much more likely to suppress our emotions, either totally or partially, as we try to produce a more socially acceptable response. The result of this management of emotion is that the anger doesn't really dissipate, and the hormones continue to surge around the body. This results in a range of symptoms affecting the entire body:

Symptom	Why Does it Occur?
Aching limbs	The build-up of glucose in the limbs can make our arms and legs feel heavy and tired. In addition, we tend to tense our muscles in preparation for flight or fight, and this tension causes pain.
Headache	Increased blood supply to the brain enables us to think more clearly, but a build-up causes a headache.
Neckache	We tend to tense our neck muscles when stressed, causing pain.
Tiredness	We feel tired because we have been burning up so much extra energy.
Dry mouth	The flow of saliva to the mouth is reduced.
Stomachache/ butterflies	Blood is diverted away from this area so digestive mechanisms are impaired; this can lead to digestive problems and discomfort.
Dizziness	Although we breathe more quickly when we're feeling angry or emotional, we tend to take shallower breaths and thus we don't inhale as much oxygen as when we're calm. This can lead to a slightly reduced supply to the brain, causing dizziness.

Feeling and suppressing anger have specifically been linked to a variety of health complaints including job stress, heart disease, high blood pressure, and anxiety. Even expressing anger is thought to be highly stress inducing; despite commonly held views that it's cathartic to release anger.

The Hostile Heart

Studies have consistently shown that chronic hostility is a particularly unhealthy emotion. Anger and hostility are significantly associated with both a higher risk of coronary heart disease in otherwise healthy individuals and poorer outcomes in patients with existing heart disease.

One example is a 2007 study by Steven Boyle and colleagues at Duke University Medical Center. The team investigated the effects of hostility within Vietnam veterans who were part of a longer-term study on the effects of "Agent Orange." It found that those who are hostile and prone to frequent and intense feelings of anger and depression could be harming their immune systems and putting themselves at risk of coronary heart disease, as well as related disorders such as type 2 diabetes and high blood pressure.

Another study from the Harvard School of Public Health looked at hostility in men and found that those with higher rates of hostility not only had poorer pulmonary function (breathing problems), but also experienced higher rates of decline as they aged.

wrath of god: anger in religion

Examples of the so-called "wrath of God" can be found in many places within religious scriptures: one instance is in the Book of Numbers, which is common to the Christian Old Testament and the Jewish Torah: "And the Lord's anger was kindled against Israel" (Numbers 32:13). But what do the religions of the world advise their followers when it comes to the anger of mere mortals?

Anger and the Ancients

The emotion of anger was dealt with extensively by ancient religions, and features in myths and legends about many of the Greek and Roman gods and heroes. One of the best-known examples of Greek literature, Homer's *Iliad*, for example, focuses on the wrath of Achilles and opens with the line: "The rage—sing it, goddess, that of Peleus's son Achilles: accursed rage, which laid countless woes upon the Achaeans."

Clearly, the role of anger was acknowledged by Greek mythology and indeed, the Greek philosopher Aristotle famously expounded his own theory of the nature of anger that is still used as inspiration for anger-management experts around the world today: "Anybody can become angry, that is easy; but to be angry with the right person, and to the right degree, and at the right time, and for the right purpose, and in the right way, that is not within everybody's power, that is not easy."

The Romans, too, talked a great deal about anger, preoccupied as they were with avoiding incurring the wrath of their gods (who included Mars, the god of terror, anger, and rage). The Roman philosopher Seneca argued in his treatise *On Anger* that we should never make a decision on the basis of anger or, for that matter, any other emotion.

Anger and Today's Religions

Most of the religions of the world concur with these early attitudes toward anger and, indeed, there seems to be widespread, cross-religious agreement, on how it ought to be dealt with.

- Islam regards anger as an emotion that must be controlled. It is commonly reported within Islamic writings that Muhammad, the emissary of Allah, said: "The man is not a good wrestler; the strong man is in fact the person who controls himself at the time of anger." (From the *Sahih al-Bukhari*, a collection of translated anecdotes about Muhammad and the founders of Islam.)

- Judaism, like Islam, holds that extreme displays of anger are unbecoming. For example, the 12th-century Jewish sage Maimonides commented that "Those who live with rage, their lives aren't worth living, therefore, they commanded [us] to distance ourselves from anger to the point where we will not be sensitive to that which is worth being angry about. This is the best way, and the way of the righteous."

- Sikhism regards anger as one of the Five Evils to guard against, and followers are repeatedly warned about the dangers of wrath, rage, and anger. Guru Arjan, one of the Ten Gurus of Sikhism, advises, "Do not be angry with any one; search your own self and live in the world with humility."

- Hinduism regards anger as "packed with more evil power than even desire" and the Hindu Dharma, a book that contains English translations of certain invaluable and engrossing speeches of Shri Chandrashekarendra Saraswati (dating from between 1907 and 1994), advises that "We must be extremely wary of this terrible sinner called anger."

- Buddhism seems to go even further in its condemnation of anger, which is listed as one of the "five hindrances." The Dalai Lama commented that "Buddhism in general teaches that anger is a destructive emotion and although anger might have some positive effects in terms of survival or moral outrage, I do not accept anger of any kind as a virtuous emotion nor aggression as constructive behavior."

- Christianity, or at least some denominations, list anger as one of the Seven Deadly Sins; indeed, anger is one of the few emotions that the Bible says Jesus specifically spoke out against. Yet Christianity, like most religions, does accept the notion of "righteous indignation," with Paul declaring to the Ephesian Christians, "Be angry, and yet do not sin." (Ephesians 4:25)

Are Religious People Less Angry, Then?

There is some evidence to suggest they are! One 1983 study by S. Philip Morgan suggested that religious people are less likely to get angry, possibly because they get less resentful if things don't go their way, and they don't intensely dislike as many people. A later study published by the sociologist Scott Schieman in 1999 found that religious involvement contributes to lower anger in older adults. It might well be then that religious people do take onboard the teachings of their spiritual leaders when it comes to anger and its management.

managing anger and mastering self

When something makes us angry our mental processes engage the anger response. This will begin with an appraisal process that evaluates the trigger to establish whether it's something that has violated our expectations, blocked our attempts at doing something, or in any other way is something we feel shouldn't have occurred.

The appraisal system will then engage the appropriate level of the anger response to kick in. But there are several ways to disrupt the anger response:

1. Engage in incompatible behavior: Anger is a state of arousal and it's impossible to experience this if you're relaxed. So, if you're able to engage in an activity that makes you feel relaxed, it will not be easy for you to feel anger at the same intensity. One way to achieve a general state of increased relaxation is by learning the skill of "deep muscle relaxation" (see opposite).
2. Do something distracting: This is a technique aimed at distracting yourself from the anger stimulus and thus reducing the intensity of the anger response.
3. Use "thought-stopping": This is another cognitive or mental technique that involves you "catching" the anger response processes and interrupting them. When you feel your anger rising you interrupt the anger response by telling yourself to stop the thoughts from going around your head.

Self-Talk Statements
The use of "self-talk statements" is a cognitive strategy aimed at increasing tolerance of the anger-eliciting event, reducing the effect that the event has, or mobilizing other coping strategies. Examples of commonly used self-talk statements include:

1. Increasing tolerance of the anger-eliciting event:
   • Worse things can happen.
   • My anger will pass.

2. Reducing the effect that the event has:
   • If I put this event into the context of my life, it's not worth getting upset about.
   • Will I remember this event in five years, or even one year?
   • My health is more important than this, so I'm not going to let it get to me.

3. Mobilizing other coping strategies:
   • I don't have to let this bother me—I can choose how to react.
   • Letting this go isn't a sign of weakness.

Channeling Anger

In trying to manage, control, and reduce our own anger, it's easy to lose sight of the benefits it can have. Anger is a valuable motivating emotion and, when channeled appropriately, can have great benefits. Parents who have lost children to disease, the relatives of murder victims, victims of injustice, many have channeled their anger into campaigns aimed at improving conditions for others or preventing such things happening again. Anger, when channeled properly, can be the driving force behind positive change.

When we're very angry it's hard to be rational and objective, but if we're to channel the anger rationality is essential. Channeling the anger is about turning what has happened into some kind of positive outcome, either for you as a wronged individual, or for the "greater good" of humankind (or at least those people in your organization). Anger can be channeled by looking at ways to implement change via letters, campaigns, demonstrations, meetings, and so on. Sometimes when we stop being angry, we lose interest in whatever made us angry in the first place. Sometimes, it can be more productive not to "let it go."

Progressive Relaxation

Here's a quick version of a technique known as "progressive relaxation." The key is to tense and relax the key muscle groups rather than every part of your body:

• Start off by tensing and relaxing your arms (including fists, biceps, and forearms).
• Next move to your back and stomach (tensing and relaxing once or twice).
• Finish with your legs (including toes and calves).

It's also useful to use a trigger word such as "relax." This can act as a kind of Pavlovian trigger to relaxation because you can learn to associate the word with the state of relaxation.

coping with the anger of others

We seem to be getting angrier and angrier—possibly as a result of increased stress, overcrowding, and higher general expectations. The consequence of this is that we're more likely than ever to encounter "Mr. or Ms. Angry," whether at work, in the superstore, or on the bus. Having some techniques up our sleeves for managing the anger of other people is always reassuring.

Techniques fall into three main areas: use of body language, speaking assertively, and using specific defusion strategies.

Using Your Body Language
Sensitivity to your body language can make the difference between calming your "opponent" down, and further antagonizing them. For example, standing face-to-face is viewed as confrontational, as is standing too close (invading someone's personal space). Touching someone who is angry (for example, putting your hand on their shoulder) should be avoided as this can often escalate conflict.

Tilting the head back can give the impression of superiority so try to keep your head straight, and never point at your opponent or jab your finger toward them.

Using Assertion Skills
Many people, when faced with rage and anger from someone else, respond by getting angry or even aggressive themselves. If someone shouts at us, we might shout back louder. If they start verbally abusing us, we become abusive back, and so on. Such behavior only serves to escalate the anger and does little to defuse the situation.

Being assertive, not aggressive, can turn the situation around. Being assertive starts with a clear observation of what the other person is doing, and what effect this is having on you; for example: "You're shouting really loudly and this is making me feel very uncomfortable." Then ask them to stop the behavior that you find inappropriate: "Please stop shouting…" Follow this swiftly by refocusing them on what they're trying to achieve (to avoid them focusing on the behavior that you are trying to prevent). To continue the example: "… and tell me, without shouting, what I've done to upset you."

Defusion Strategies
Defusion strategies are words and actions that can take the wind out of the sails of an angry person. Not all the techniques described below will work all of the time; it's about selecting the most appropriate one, while bearing in mind that sometimes nothing will defuse the situation.

1. Apologize: There is nothing as likely to stop anger in its tracks like an apology. Of course, this should only be used if it's appropriate to apologize; in other words, if an admission of regret is not detrimental to your cause. But, if it's at all possible, an apology can really take the sting out of an angry situation.

2. Diversion techniques: If apologizing and sympathizing are not appropriate, distraction or diversion techniques may be called for. This family of techniques relies on introducing change to defuse a situation.

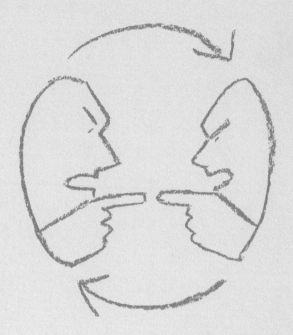

There are two main possible changes that can be utilized: changing the topic under discussion, or changing the environment in some way. Changing the topic can create confusion, which can momentarily halt the escalating anger, giving you both the space to move on more calmly.

Changing the environment can be achieved by suggesting a move to another office, to a place where there are people present, or where there are no other people around. Gaining or eliminating an audience can change the need of the aggressor to be angry, but even just changing the environment slightly (sitting down rather than standing) can change the focus enough to introduce a bit of calm.

How Good Are You at Defusing Anger?

As honestly as you can, see if you agree with the following statements:

- If someone gets angry, I tend to get angry too.
- When someone, for example, my child or partner, starts shouting, I find my own voice rising.
- I rarely apologize, even if I'm in the wrong.
- I often point or jab my finger toward people when I'm angry.
- If I'm accused of something, I tend to react by making a counter-accusation.

Author's Comments

If you agree with a lot of the above statements, then you might need to look carefully at improving the way you manage the anger of other people.

Chapter 6

sadness and joy

measuring happiness

Most people in developed countries are more economically prosperous now than at any point in history, but are we any happier? Do we even know what makes us happy?

The answer to the second question is that we have a fair idea. The General Social Survey in the United States and the European Union's Eurobarometer have run every other year for over 25 years. Both of these ask questions on happiness, as does the World Values Survey—an international effort by social scientists that started in 1981. There is even the World Database of Happiness run by Professor Ruut Veenhoven at the University of Rotterdam.

What Makes Us Happy?

The big problem with the question of what makes us happy is that it depends on what the situation is. For example, although we may enjoy our food in prosperous countries, it's rarely rated as a significant source of happiness; yet a lack of food could make us very unhappy.

The British economist, Richard Layard, has used the wealth of research data to identify the "big seven" happiness factors. These are:

- family relationships
- financial situation
- work status (job security)
- community and friends
- health
- personal freedom
- personal values.

The biggest single indicator is family relationships. It seems that married people are happiest, followed by (in order of happiness) those who are cohabiting, widowed, single, divorced, and separated. On a happiness scale of one to ten, there is a difference of almost one point between married and separated people.

Unemployment and job insecurity can knock up to half a point off a person's happiness score, and if your health drops by one point on a five-point scale you can lose another half a point from your total happiness.

The concept of "personal values" relates to having meaning in your life, and this is a consistent theme in theories and data on happiness. Layard reports that people who believe in God tend to score, on average, a third of a point higher on the happiness scale.

Males and females are about as happy as each other, and even though some phases of life seem to be more stressful than others, age does not appear to affect happiness.

So what about money? It would be nice to say that it's not related to happiness, but this doesn't seem to be the case. Within most countries, rich people are happier than poor people, and the populations of richer countries seem to be happier than those of poorer ones. However, this isn't a consistent relationship—in spite of being about a third of the way down most measures of wealth, Veenhoven places Mexico in the top five happy countries; though there is little agreement in the area of measuring happiness and other indices place it much lower. But there is a general trend, with the least happy countries tending to be very poor. However, although most countries have been growing richer and richer, the average level of happiness does not seem to have increased greatly.

How Do You Get Happier?

So will getting more money make you happier? The answer seems to be "no." You'll probably feel quite high for a while, but then you'll likely return to your original level of happiness. Psychologist Ed Diener, of the University of Illinois, notes that happiness is quite a stable trait, changing little from year to year. Major life events such as widowhood can change your overall level of happiness, but psychologist Martin Seligman suggests that there is typically about 10–15 percent variation in your basic level of happiness at most.

To some extent happiness is a personal thing; what makes one person happy will not necessarily make someone else happy. But good relationships, health, and having a meaning to your life beyond making money are generally recognized as being the most important factors.

So How Happy Are You?

There are countless ways of defining and measuring happiness, but Ed Diener, one of the leading experts on happiness (he is known as "Dr. Happy" in the psychological community), maintains that the best way is to ask someone how happy he or she is on a scale of one to ten.

So, applying Ed Diener's happiness scale, how happy are you?

Happiest and Least Happy

World Database of Happiness*	Satisfaction with Life **
Top Five	
Iceland	Costa Rica
Denmark	Norway
Colombia	Ireland
Switzerland	Denmark
Mexico	Canada
Bottom Five	
Belarus	Benin
Chad	Burundi
Togo	Zimbabwe
Zimbabwe	Togo
Tanzania	Tanzania

	Selected Others	
8th	Australia	7th
12th	Canada	6th
18th	New Zealand	11th
25th	United Kingdom	9th
27th	United States	23rd

* Average happiness in 144 nations 2000–8

** Data compiled in the New Economic Foundation's *Happy Planet Index 2.0*, 2009

Author's Comments

Ruut Veenhoven reports average happiness scores of around seven for English-speaking Western countries. Australia scores relatively highly with an average of 7.7. Ed Diener's team have found that most people report being happy most of the time, though few report consistently high levels of happiness.

forms of depression

We all experience sadness at some point or other in our life, and may have periods when life seems less fun. Depression, however, is a clinical condition in which the feeling of sadness and the loss of pleasure become unbearable and persistent. It's one of the most prevalent illnesses in the world and has been recognized by the World Health Organization as the leading cause of disability when measured by "years lost to disability." Some estimate that up to 17 percent of Americans will suffer from depression at some point in their life.

Major Depression

By far the most common form of depression is "major depression." Characterized by feelings of sadness, in this state all appetites are reduced and normal pleasures fail to satisfy. Lethargy and agitation are common, making concentration and creativity impossible, while thoughts tend to be negative and pessimistic.

Rates of depression vary around the world, tending to be more common in the West than in the East, but one finding is highly consistent: women are two to three times more likely to be affected than men. The reasons for this, however, are not clear. It's been noted that younger males are more likely externalize negative feelings than younger women, so women are more likely to beat themselves up where men will choose a different target. Others suggest that traditional female roles of submissiveness and dependency make it easier for depression to be accepted in and by women so it's more likely to be admitted but less likely to be addressed. Psychologist Susan Nolen-Hoeksema, at Yale, has noted that women are more prone than men to "ruminating." Whereas men will tend to find a distraction from their concerns, women are more likely to think them through over and over again, and so-called ruminators are more likely to become depressed.

Bipolar Disorder

Bipolar disorder (once known as "manic depression") is characterized by the bouts of mania that precede the depressive episodes. Intense elation, enormous self-confidence, and a constant rush of ideas and the energy to push them forward are all present. People experiencing bipolar disorder can sometimes be productive, although their failure to test reality means that much of what they set out to achieve can founder.

Mania without a following depressive phase is very rare, yet some feel the ensuing depression is a price worth paying for the elation and creativity they experience. The illness is often associated with such creative individuals as Tchaikovsky, van Gogh, and the poets Tennyson and Shelley.

Bipolar disorder is far less common than major depression, affecting around 1 percent of people and with no gender differential.

What Causes Depression?

The diathesis–stress model is popular as an explanation of many mental disorders. This states that some people—for reasons genetic, biological, or experiential—are more prone to the illness than others, but that it's triggered by a particular stress.

This first bout of depression, typically occurring in adolescence or young adulthood, often seems to be triggered by a life event; subsequent bouts may occur without such a conspicuous cause. Some have suggested that this "kindling" effect may be because the first experience makes the brain sensitive to the condition, increasing proneness to it.

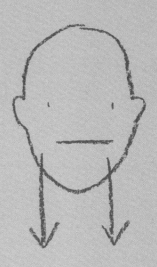

Depression and Suicide

Apart from being extremely unpleasant and debilitating for the sufferer, depression also carries the risk of suicide. However, there is a great deal of misinformation surrounding suicide; which of the following do you think are true?

1. People who talk about committing suicide don't generally do it.

2. A person will generally appear to be quite desperate and depressed before they attempt suicide.

3. If you think someone is suicidal, talking to them about it will make them more likely to try it.

4. If a person tries but fails to commit suicide, they probably didn't want to die.

5. It's very rare for people to consider suicide.

Answers

They're all false. People who are suicidal are often quite desperate and are seeking escape, want help, or even want to taunt others. Suicide can be attempted for a variety of reasons including political action or as a calmly rationalized decision. Ignoring the risk of suicide will not make it go away. A failure to commit suicide may be because the person lacks information on how to do it (females are more likely to attempt suicide, though males are more likely to actually die—this may be because they tend to use more violent and effective methods). Research suggests that 40–80 percent of people consider suicide at some point in their life.

vicious cycles of depressive cognition

Mood or "affective" disorders are characterized by feelings of sadness or elation and the failure to experience pleasure. Not surprisingly, much of the focus on the causes and cures of these illnesses has been on the way people feel. But what if the key actually lies in the way they think?

American psychiatrist Aaron Beck has been one of the most influential contributors to the field of depression. We commonly perceive our mood as affecting our ability to think, to make objective evaluations and balanced decisions. But Beck suggests that it's actually the way we think that leads to, and maintains, depressive disorders. The feelings of sadness and loss of pleasure may be the things that a depressed person most readily identifies in his or her illness, but to the outside observer it's often more obvious that the sufferer has become pessimistic—attending to the negative and ignoring the positive.

The Negative Schemata

Schemata are ways of seeing something, the whole bundle of thoughts and feelings that is automatically triggered when a particular idea or concept comes to mind. For example, to one person the word "camping" instantly summons images of freedom, fresh air, good friends, and a better way of life. To another (me, for example) the flood of thoughts is of damp and cold, tiredness, unpleasant food, and even the most basic of tasks becoming tiresome and difficult. My "schema" of camping is a negative one and is based, to be honest, on two moderately bad (and no good) experiences of it. I've no doubt that if I tried it again I might like it. But what if that schema was something more fundamental to my life, and more deeply ingrained?

Beck suggests that people who suffer from depression have strong negative schemata about more fundamental issues. This might be an "ineptness" schema about themselves: "Everything I do goes wrong." Or a self-blame schema: "Everything that goes wrong is my fault." It would be hard to feel positive with these thoughts. They could make everything a burden.

Cognitive Biases

Alongside the negative schemata, those who suffer from depression may have irrational ways of thinking about things. These are called "cognitive biases." A depressed person might base negative conclusions on no evidence whatsoever, or select only the negative evidence from the midst of a wealth of positive signs. I have often seen clients reject or forget every piece of positive feedback they receive, while focusing on one or two areas in which they did less well. They take this as conclusive proof that they are failures.

The Negative Triad

Beck believes that in those who suffer from depression these schemata and cognitive biases combine with a "negative triad": an over-arching negative view of self, of the future, and of their ability to cope with their environment.

If you put these three together you are set up to receive negative feedback from every situation, to expect everything to work against you, and to be incapable of anticipating any joy or release from this position. Fundamentally, it is depressing.

Cognitive Behavioral Therapy

One of the most widely used approaches to dealing with depression is cognitive behavioral therapy (CBT). The sufferer is taught to evaluate the thought process, identify the negative patterns, and learn new ones. This is the "cognitive" component, which deals with the way they think.

The "behavioral" element is to start acting in a more positive way, doing the things that non-depressed people do in the ways that they do them. This may seem artificial, but it helps reinforce the growing perception of being a healthy person who can cope with the world.

Do You Think Positively or Negatively?

Think of three different situations in which you have been unsuccessful. Now ask yourself the three following questions about each situation.

1. Was it a) mainly your fault; or, b) caused by other factors?
2. If that type of situation arose again, would a) everything be pretty much the same; or, b) things be different?
3. Is it due to a) something that generally applies; or, b) something specific about that particular situation?

Author's Comments

If you have tended to answer "a," then it may be that you expect things to go wrong, and you don't see yourself as someone who can make them right. There may be something comical about the person who repeats the mantra "Every day in every way I am getting better and better," but they're actually thinking positively about themselves and picturing themselves as a healthy developing person. Try it—it can actually work!

death and mourning

The death of someone close to you is undoubtedly one of the saddest experiences you'll have to face in your life. Some estimates suggest that about one third of all psychotherapy is related to the death of a loved one. There are great cultural differences in the way people view death and respond to it, but some psychologists suggest there are also some universal elements.

The Kübler-Ross Stages

Several different models of the mourning process have been proposed, but the most famous of these is the Kübler-Ross DABDA model; standing for denial, anger, bargaining, depression, and acceptance. It was created by Elizabeth Kübler-Ross to describe the different stages of grief and mourning that can be experienced either when faced with the death of someone close or by your own impending death. However, like many such models, it has been applied widely to all sorts of loss, including job loss, relationship break-up, or even the end of a long-running television series.

In more detail, the five stages are:

- Denial: The person can't quite grasp what is happening or refuses to believe it.
- Anger: Protesting at the unfairness of the loss.
- Bargaining: The person tries to make promises, often to his or her God, in exchange for a change in circumstance.

- Depression: The stage in which the person feels a terrible sadness and grieves for what is or will be lost. At this stage the person understands what is happening but is overwhelmed by it. It may be accompanied by withdrawal from others.
- Acceptance: The hoped-for end of the process. The person is more peaceful and reconciled, though he or she may not have strong positive or negative feelings.

Some models include guilt as an important component. Mourners can sometimes feel a slight sense of relief at a person's death, as any problems with the relationship will have gone away. Guilt at having these feelings, as well as guilt about unkind thoughts, words, or deeds, unresolved issues, and things that have been left unsaid, can be a significant source of sorrow.

Like all models that present mourning in stages, the Kübler-Ross model has been criticized for suggesting that a person will, or even should, move through all these stages.

A common complaint is that people who don't experience one of these stages may feel that they have not mourned properly, and may even be judged by others for it. Elizabeth Kübler-Ross herself pointed out that she didn't expect that everyone would experience all of these stages, nor that they would necessarily come in this order.

Death and Culture

These criticisms are not limited to psychological models of mourning, as many people feel that their own or others' mourning is somehow not as it should be. For example, many worry that they haven't cried or felt sufficient sadness, or haven't left it long enough before getting on with their lives.

Clear cultural practices on how a person should mourn may seem restrictive to some, but to others they give a clear signal of what is expected—giving them one less thing to worry about. These practices also put responsibilities on those around the mourners to make the process easier.

What Should I Feel?

Mourning can be a very disorientating process. Apart from losing a significant person in your life, it can also signal major changes to your role, your social contacts, and your income. People may find it hard to approach you because they don't know what to say or how to help you (the received wisdom is that listening or even sitting quietly is better than saying things, anyway), and on top of all this you may have a rush of extreme emotions—or you may not.

Different people have different emotional profiles, and the circumstances around the death, your own beliefs, and the relationship you had with the deceased can all have a major impact. Those with a faith and those who feel they have a meaning to their life tend, on average, to have a quicker and less intense mourning than others. Those for whom the death of a loved one was unexpected, such as in an accident, can often have a longer and more difficult mourning process.

There may also be cultural and religious prescriptions about how emotions should be expressed. Some Islamic, Sikh, and Hindu teachings suggest that grief should be freely shown but restrained, wheras others expect the mourner to be more demonstrative.

the laughter cure

Laughter appears to be quite universal: even children who are deaf and blind laugh naturally. This suggests it's not something we learn but is innate.

What Makes You Laugh?

Your first response might be a television show such as *The Simpsons* or a funny person like John Cleese. However, humor only accounts for about 20 percent of our laughter. Psychologist Robert R. Provine and his colleagues at the University of Maryland found that most laughter happens in normal social exchanges. Simple statements like "Hi John!" and "Can I get you a drink?" are frequently interspersed with laughter. In the absence of books, films, and the like, you are 30 times more likely to laugh when you are with other people than when you are on your own.

Of course, there are other causes of laughter, and they don't have to be pleasant. Nervousness, whether because of fear or discomfort, can make you laugh; on the other hand, so can a feeling of great euphoria. If all else fails, tickling will make people laugh, even if they don't want to.

Laugh and the World Laughs with You

Laughter certainly seems to be contagious. That's why so many comedy programs have laughter accompanying them. Provine reports that these "laughter tracks," whether from a live audience or pre-recorded, make a show seem funnier. Unsurprisingly, the laughter alone is not enough, you do need the joke too, but with the joke in place you can make the audience laugh more and believe the show to be funnier by giving them laughter cues.

The most famous case of contagious laughter occurred in Tanganyika (now Tanzania) in 1962. Pupils at an all-girls school began to giggle; when the teacher tried to calm the class down, they didn't seem able to stop. The laughter spread throughout the school and to the broader community as the girls headed home. Despite everyone's efforts, the laughter didn't stop and within a couple of weeks the Red Cross was called in and the school had to be closed. The situation took months to resolve.

Is Laughter Good for You?

There is a popular belief that laughter is good for you. It can certainly make you feel happier and take your mind off your worries, but there is also evidence that it's good for your health.

Numerous studies have shown that laughter can be a powerful aid in managing pain. People distracted with humor can experience less pain: some hospitals now routinely use humor before painful injections, particularly with children. This may not seem especially surprising, but laughter can also help reduce heart disease by expanding the inner lining of the artery walls (the endothelium), so boosting blood flow by up to 20 percent. A study showed that blood flow was increased in 95 percent of those who were shown a clip from a funny movie, whereas 70 percent of those who saw a stressful clip experienced reduced blood flow.

Laughter also boosts the immune system, increasing the activation of cells that fight infection. It can reduce the amount of stress hormone in your system and even help reduce allergic symptoms.

On the other hand, laughter isn't always good for you. The Greek stoic philosopher Chrysippus (c.280–207 BCE) was reputed to have died laughing as he watched his drunken donkey. Overall, though, the evidence seems to suggest that laughter really is good for you.

Wanted: Good Sense of Humor

A study by Karl Grammer and Irenäus Eibl-Eibesfeldt found that when men and women meet there is a relationship between how interested they are in each other and how much laughter there is in the conversation. However, for both males and females, their level of interest was related to how much time the woman spent laughing, not the man.

Is Animal Laughter Contagious?

Provine identified a standard pattern to human laughter. It is characterized by repeated syllables with broadly the same gap between each syllable and a set frequency range; for example, "ho ho ho" or "ha ha ha," which only vary with the first or last syllable in the laugh. This enables us to recognize the incredible range of noises that people make when they laugh, from a chuckle through guffaws to the "evil laugh" beloved of cartoon villains.

Animals also seem to laugh—some monkeys make a panting noise when tickled or when playing with their fellows. Even rats produce a high-pitched noise when tickled, which suggests that this may be their form of laughter. But because they don't follow the same patterns as human laughter, you're unlikely to find yourself giggling uncontrollably when you hear a rat squeaking with glee.

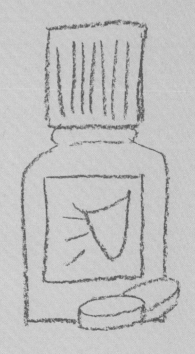

martin seligman

For a long time, Martin Seligman's name was associated with depression and hopelessness, but today he is a champion of happiness in psychology. Here's how it happened…

Depressing Dogs
Imagine a dog locked in a compartment with two sections. A light begins to flash and a few seconds later he gets a mild electric shock in his paws. Quite sensibly, he runs away. Arriving in the other section of the compartment he finds that the floor there isn't electrified. He soon works out that when the light flashes it's a good time to flee to the second section.

There's nothing particularly surprising here—except that a psychologist can make a good living electrocuting dogs!—and dogs will generally work out how to avoid the shocks.

But Seligman and his colleagues found that you could, in effect, train a dog to give up and make no attempt to escape. All he had to do was put the dog in a compartment in which both sections of the floor were electrified. The dog, unable to avoid the inevitable, eventually stopped trying and surrendered to his fate. Now, when you put him in the original compartment, he seems unable to learn that he can escape the shock by moving to the other section. Even when the experimenter carries him to the safe section he still doesn't learn. When the light flashes he just sits there, whining, without the will to save himself.

You may have met people who act a bit like that dog, and Seligman noted that many people with depression become very passive, losing the motivation to act. He called this condition, in which a sense of having no control leads to a passive state, "learned helplessness."

The Power of Optimism
Seligman makes an interesting observation about his dogs. He found that although some dogs were helpless even before the experiments began, about a third never learned to become helpless. He again noticed similarities with people and began to investigate what it was that protected these individuals, and the answer is "optimism." When faced with difficult situations, some people tend to blame themselves, accept there is little they can do, and assume that things are unlikely to change. These people are far more likely to develop helplessness than those who put their difficulties down to external factors, who believe they can have an impact, and who decide that this is not going to be the pattern of things to come.

also found that these optimists had better immune systems, were less likely to t depression, and that they emed to live longer too.

sitive Psychology
st forward to the present d Professor Seligman is e director of the Positive ychology Center in nnsylvania. He has scribed his realization that ychology as a discipline, oted so much as it is in ental illness and dysfunction, s a very negative flavor.

hat if, rather than focusing ainly on making people ffer less, it put more energy o finding out how to make troubled people's lives even tter and more productive?

This "positive psychology" movement is now a major force within psychology. We've long been able to classify illness and suffering, but Seligman can now present a model of "character strengths and virtues" that seems to be consistent across 70 different countries and a wide range of cultures. Psychology has come a long way in helping people not to be depressed; now there is some hope that it can even help us be happier.

Be Nice and Live Longer

Seligman recommends making something called a "gratitude visit." Think of a living person who has made a positive difference in your life. Now write 300 words explaining what they did, how it affected you, and where you are now. The next step is to give them a call and ask if you can have a few minutes of their time, but don't tell them what for.

When you arrive on their doorstep, sit them down and read out your 300 words. I understand it is a good idea to take some tissues with you.

This isn't just a "nice" thing to do. Seligman's research suggests that those making even one such visit, when followed up at a later date, reported higher levels of happiness and lower levels of depression.

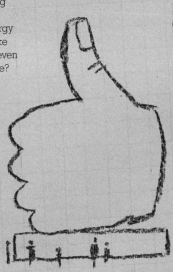

a happiness called flow

I still recall that first time my guitar playing really came together. Oblivious to everything around me, I was totally immersed in the music, a strange blend of concentration and effortlessness. I was in a state that psychologists call "flow."

Flow is a concept identified by psychologist Mihaly Csikszentmihalyi (pronounced chick-sent-me-high-ee). He first noticed it in painters, who seemed to go into a trance as they focused totally on their task. It's a state within which you are fully immersed in what you're doing, and the challenge of the task almost perfectly matches your ability to complete it.

Csikszentmihalyi called the state "flow," as so many of those who experienced it likened it to being carried along by a current. Flow is distinct from pleasure, because pleasure doesn't necessarily imply activity; for example, you might derive pleasure from a favorite television show or relaxing listening to music, both of which are passive activities. Flow, on the other hand, involves being actively engaged, and has a goal.

There are a number of key elements to flow, although not all of them need to be present for the experience to be considered as such. These include:

1. A goal: In contrast to the complex and competing demands of our daily lives, the flow experience has a clear and focused goal.

2. The right challenge: The task is neither too hard nor too easy.

3. No distractions: Nothing intrudes on your attention, there are no worries, and you are focused purely on the task in hand.

4. Just do it: You don't reflect on or appraise what you are doing; you just get on with doing it.

5. Live for the moment: You are focused on the here and now, without considering what has been or what will be.

6. Time becomes distorted: Often you can lose track of time and hours pass without you noticing. On other occasions time may slow so every detail becomes emphasized.

7. The activity is "autotelic": The activity is valued for what it is, it is not merely a means to an end but the end in itself.

Was That Fun?

When my six-year-old son makes a challenging jigsaw, he is totally immersed, humming noisily to himself but with an extremely serious look on his face. You would never guess he was actually enjoying it, but as soon as he sits up to view it you can see the satisfaction on his face. This is because although flow is an important source of enjoyment, satisfaction, and happiness, you may not be aware that you're happy while you are experiencing it. You may even find the process uncomfortable or painful (perhaps something like rock climbing is a more appropriate example than a jigsaw), but after the event you will look back at it as having been fun.

When Does Flow Happen?

Csikszentmihalyi reports that about 15 percent of people have never experienced flow, whereas 15–20 percent experience it every day. He believes you can maximize your happiness and productivity by identifying where flow happens for you and indulging in these activities while trying to bring flow into all aspects of your life.

I recall talking to a soldier who had been involved in fierce street fighting. I asked him if it was as chaotic as it looked on television. He told me how his training had kicked in; he was doing what he was good at, within a team he fully trusted. The fear disappeared as he became immersed in his task. He knew people who had died there and was aware of the horror of it all, but there was no mistaking the satisfaction in his voice as he talked about his experience.

A key component of flow is that it is the process that matters, rather than the result. Csikszentmihalyi noticed that painters might spend five minutes viewing the picture when it was finished, but then they put it away to get on with the next canvas. Nobody does a jigsaw because they want the picture that comes out at the end—the point of doing a jigsaw is just that: to be doing it.

Much that is written on flow relates to creative activities and sport. Musicians call it being "in the groove"; for sportspeople it's being "in the zone," where the game becomes everything and the conscious and unconscious mind work effortlessly with the trained body. But it can also be applied to all aspects of life and Csikszentmihalyi encourages us to seek out ways of bringing as many aspects of our life into flow as possible.

the anatomy of joy

Often when we refer to "happiness" we think of a level of contentment and pleasure, but there is also a more intense experience that we might refer to as joy, ecstasy, or euphoria. It's less common and more short-lived than day-to-day happiness. The words we use to describe it often have spiritual origins or connotations: "ecstasy" comes from the Greek *ekstasis*, meaning "standing outside oneself," and relates to transcending your physical self; whereas "enthusiasm" originates in the concept of being possessed by a god or spirit. Therefore it comes as no surprise that the spiritual side of such feelings is an area that psychologists have taken great interest in.

The Religious Experience

William James is often thought of as the first modern psychologist and he had a particular interest in what is known as the "mystical experience" or the "religious experience." It is a phenomenon where people feel they have an experience of the divine, often characterized by great joy and insight. In his book, *The Varieties of Religious Experience*, James quotes a contemporary of his who, traveling home in a cab one day, reported: "there came upon me a sense of exultation, of immense joyousness, accompanied or immediately followed by intellectual illumination impossible to describe."

James's studies revealed four characteristics of this type of experience:

- Passivity: The experience is not under the control of the person experiencing it.
- Ineffability: Words can never quite express the experience; a person who has such an experience often feels that attempting to explain it will do it an injustice. They believe you have to experience it to understand it.
- Noetic experience: The person feels they have learnt something or gained an insight, and what they have learned appears to have "a curious sense of authority."
- Transitoriness: The experience lasts but minutes, very rarely more than half an hour, then the person returns to their normal state.

The Physical Perspective

Some psychologists believe that the mystical experience can be explained entirely in physiological terms. For example, the magnetic stimulation of the temporal lobes in the brain is claimed to give a person the impression of an ethereal presence.

The problem, as with drug-related mystical experiences, is that we can't be absolutely certain that it's the physical stimulation of the brain that causes the sensations—it may be that it simply reduces inhibitions that create barriers with the spiritual, which is the belief of many of those cultures that have used drugs in religious rituals.

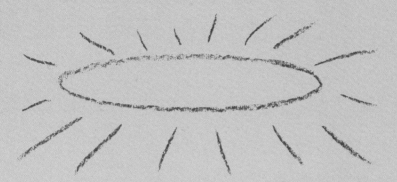

The effects of these experiences are generally long-lasting and can change lives. They can be initiated by a number of things including religious rituals, praying, chanting, dance, music, and pain; or they can happen entirely spontaneously. People generally report feelings of great joy and wellbeing, although such an experience can nevertheless be unnerving or frightening. These experiences appear to be quite universal, appearing in different cultures and religions. They vary in their intensity and some studies suggest that almost 50 percent of people experience one of some sort at some point in their life.

The Mystical Experience and Psychosis

People suffering from psychotic illnesses can feel great joy, hear voices, believe they are influenced by external agencies, and have great insights that others will not be able to appreciate. So why isn't the mystical experience simply a form of madness?

The key distinctions between the mystical experience and psychosis is that the former often appears to be entirely consistent with good mental health; thought processes are not disturbed, those experiencing it find it very rewarding and beneficial despite its unusualness, and there appear to be no negative after-effects.

The Drug Effect

Many researchers discount mystical experiences initiated by drugs because the effect may be due purely to the drug. Although many religions such as Islam and Christianity have taboos against intoxication, others routinely use drugs such as peyote, cannabis, and hallucinogenic mushrooms in their religious rituals.

Walter Pahnke was a minister and physician who conducted experiments into the effects of hallucinogenic drugs such as LSD before they had developed their current reputation. In one study in 1962, he gave pills to 20 divinity students during their Good Friday worship. Ten had received a placebo and only one of these had a religious experience. The pills for the remaining ten contained psilocybin, a powerful psychedelic, and almost all of these had mystical experiences. In a follow-up, a quarter of a century later, those who had the psilocybin reported that it differed from later non-drug-induced religious experiences, but was valued nonetheless.

Chapter 7

fear and excitement

anxiety disorders

It's said that we live in an increasingly stressful world; but for many of us the everyday danger of attack by animals or others, the fear of going without food or being bitten by something poisonous, has all but disappeared. Yet sociologist Ronald C. Kessler and his colleagues at Harvard Medical School estimate that almost a quarter of all Americans will suffer an anxiety disorder at some point in their lives.

Panic Attacks

A common symptom for most people suffering from an anxiety disorder is the panic attack. Although one typically lasts only a few minutes, it can be quite terrifying and debilitating. If you were unlucky enough to suffer from one you might feel dizzy, weak, and disorientated, your heart thumping and your mouth dry. You could get chest pains, sweating and trembling, and a terrible feeling of fear and doom. Many sufferers fear they are going mad, that they are going to faint or even die. Yet often there is no obvious cause, or the fear of the attack itself is the only reason for it.

A study by American psychologist David H. Barlow suggests that each year, 10 percent of otherwise healthy Americans will suffer at least one panic attack.

Types of Anxiety

Anxiety disorders are normally broken up into the following main types:

- Phobia: A terrible fear of a specific thing or situation (of which there are a huge variety, from snakes to public places).
- Obsessive-compulsive disorder (OCD): The experience of persistent and recurring irrational thoughts and the need to carry out repetitive, sometimes ritualistic actions such as counting to a hundred, or touching a number of objects in your bedroom in a strict sequence.
- Post-traumatic stress disorder (PTSD): Anxiety brought on by a particular trauma—such as an accident, rape, or being in battle—that keeps recurring long after the event.
- Generalized anxiety disorder: A persistent feeling of high anxiety.
- Panic disorder: Frequent panic attacks that have no apparent cause.

Why so Anxious?

Apart from PTSD, there is often no clear reason for the panic attacks to start, but many are maintained by a vicious cycle of biological and psychological feedback. Whether an incident of panic is started by a worry or by a bodily stimulus—for example, being short of breath or feeling a little dizzy—the sufferer worries about the symptom, perhaps with thoughts like "I'm going to faint" or "Oh no, I'm having a panic attack!" This fear then stimulates the fear responses throughout the body and the fight, flight, or freeze mechanism described on pages 16–17 escalates. Adrenalin courses through the body and makes the person feel even more tense, light-headed, and uncomfortable. Noticing this causes even more concern and so the panic progresses. Although panic attacks rarely last more than ten minutes, they can leave the sufferer feeling exhausted, vulnerable, and afraid.

Psychological research has shown that people who are more focused on, and fearful of, their bodily sensations are more likely to experience panic attacks, as are those who are more fearful of losing control. Panic attacks involve unpleasant bodily sensations and threaten loss of control, as sufferers are fearful of choking or fainting or having to leave the room. As such, once a person has a panic attack the stage is set for a vicious cycle.

Relaxing with the White Bear

Get yourself a watch, a pen, and some paper. Now time yourself for two minutes, during which time you shouldn't think about a white bear. Every time you think about the white bear, make a mark on the paper. After two minutes, see how many times the white bear has come to mind.

It's quite likely that the white bear intruded into your thoughts from time to time. However, you may also find him coming to mind in the next quarter of an hour or so.

This is based on an experiment conducted by Daniel Wegner and colleagues at the Mental Control Laboratory of Harvard University. It demonstrates that, for most people, actively trying not to think about something can often bring it to mind. Further, those who try to suppress the thought will later think about it more than those who didn't try to suppress it. People with OCD in particular may invest a lot of effort in trying to suppress their negative thoughts, with the unfortunate consequence that they think about them more.

For this reason, many approaches to relaxation emphasize that a person shouldn't think about "not being afraid" because that makes you think about fear. Rather, the focus should be on "calm" and "peace."

fear or excitement

We have already seen that the same physical symptoms can be related to various emotional states. Fear and excitement are two of the closest because they both prepare the body and mind for action.

You may recall that we have schemata; whole clusters of ideas, thoughts, feelings, and images that are conjured when we think of a particular situation. When you fear something and dwell on it you incorporate fear into that schema. Suppose you're worried about giving a speech and every time you think about it you picture yourself standing there, shaking, mumbling, looking foolish, and feeling fearful. Every time you think this, you're associating fear and an inability to cope with the concept of giving a speech. You're conditioning yourself to respond with fear.

The good news is that some psychologists believe that the better you are at conditioning yourself to be afraid, the better you may be at conditioning yourself to enjoy things. After all, you have already demonstrated how much you can influence your feelings by thinking about problems.

Visualization

As a musician I used to get terrible stage-fright and I hated live performances. By constantly thinking about how much I was going to hate them, I reinforced the idea that performances were going to be unpleasant and fear-inducing. I had a particularly big concert coming up so I thought I'd apply some psychology. I spent 20 minutes a day doing visualizations using auto-hypnosis (a form of self-hypnosis that can make you more receptive to the visualization) and pictured myself enjoying every aspect of the concert.

As soon as we arrived at the venue it was like a switch had been flicked; I felt excited and very happy. Occasionally I said to myself "This is all going to go wrong soon," but I silenced that voice. It was the most enjoyable and relaxing concert I had ever played. But why wouldn't it be? By then I had convinced myself I was the kind of person who loved being on stage.

Using Visualization

There are numerous techniques for changing your automatic response to a situation and many of them use "visualization," the process of picturing yourself being effective and in control in the situation you fear.

1. Relaxation: The first stage is to become relaxed; if you are tense when you are doing your visualizations it isn't going to help. One approach is to lie down on the floor with a cushion under your head. Close your eyes and concentrate on your legs—tense them so you can feel what the tension is like, and then relax them. Do this a couple of times. Then do it for the other parts of your body. Try not to think of anything but tensing and relaxing the muscles, and keep it slow.

2. Going deeper: Now picture somewhere that you associate with feeling relaxed—the beach, some woods, whatever works for you. Think about what you'll see and hear there, the sensations on your skin, and the smells in the air. Once you have a good picture, count very slowly from ten down to one, knowing that you are getting more relaxed with every number.

3. Now you're relaxed, picture the situation you're worried about but see yourself in control, calm, maybe even enjoying it, if that is appropriate. Repeat positive phrases in your head, such as "I'm calm and relaxed"; avoid negative words such as "fear"; saying "I feel no fear" brings fear into the image, which isn't helpful. If negative images come to mind, don't worry about them, just return to the positive ones.

4. After about 15 minutes, or when you're ready, slowly open your eyes. It's a good idea to lie there for a couple of minutes before resuming your normal activities.

Warnings: Don't set an alarm clock to tell you when to finish, as it can be quite a shock if you are in a very relaxed state. You should also be aware that if you're very tired and very relaxed you could fall asleep during this process.

If your fears are having a significant effect on you it may advisable to consult your doctor.

carl jung

Freud was immensely impressed with the young Swiss psychologist and psychiatrist Carl Gustav Jung (1875–1961), hailing him as the "crown-prince" of the psychoanalytic movement. When Jung went on to found his own "analytical psychology" movement, however, Freud felt betrayed, not only at the loss of his favored follower but also because Jung's model was such a dramatic departure from Freudian orthodoxy.

Freud sees us, in essence, as machines, driven by our biological and sexual urges. For Jung we are transcendent creatures, driven by our ancestral past but also pulled forward by our potential future. Jung embraces the religion, spirituality, and mythology that had no place in Freud's understanding of humanity.

The Collective Unconscious

Like Freud, Jung believed us to have an ego, the conscious mind. Sitting below this is the "personal unconscious" (similar to Freud's preconscious), which contains all the thoughts, memories, and feelings that are available to the conscious mind but are not currently there. The memory of what you had for dinner last night is held in your personal unconscious and can be recalled now I have mentioned it.

Jung's major contribution, though, is in the third aspect of mind—the "collective unconscious." He claimed that much of what humanity experienced and learned during its evolution and distant past is retained in the human psyche. These fundamental ideas and concepts, which Jung calls "archetypes," are held in common by all people in all ages.

The Anxious Mind

Our collective unconscious gives us the potential to fear things that have been a threat, such as the dark or spiders. This potential can be triggered by particular events, thus giving rise to phobias or anxieties. For Jung these are simply exaggerated expressions of normal behaviors to be treated as they are now, rather than requiring a search for a cause within a person's past that needs to be addressed.

Health comes from harmony between the three parts of the mind. If the collective unconscious were ignored or repressed by the conscious mind, not only would this lead to an empty life, but the unconscious would begin to press in on the conscious, distorting rationality in the process.

Are You a Feeling Type?

Jung postulated four functions by which we perceive and make decisions about the world. When combined with information on whether we're introverts or extroverts, this enables us to identify a great deal about how we think and act.

Two of the four functions, "intuition" and "sensing," relate to how we perceive the world, whereas "thinking" and "feeling" relate to how we make decisions.

Try this brief questionnaire to get you thinking about whether you are a feeling type or a thinking type.

1. I can make rational decisions based entirely on the facts without letting my feelings get in the way.

2. If I have to evaluate a situation I would prefer to get involved in it to see what it is like from the inside rather than observe it from the outside.

3. Decisions should be made on the basis of objective information rather than subjective feelings.

4. My values and beliefs have a major impact on the decisions I make.

5. You can't take people's feelings too much into account when you have to make important decisions.

6. I am comfortable making a decision if it "feels right," even if the facts don't fully back it up.

Author's Comments

If you said "yes," to 2, 4, and 6 more than to 1, 3, and 5, you may be more of a feeling type than a thinking type. Thinking types like to use logic, reason, and rules. They are concerned with being impersonal, consistent, and reasonable. Feeling types are more influenced by subjective issues, their values and beliefs and are concerned with harmony and how people feel.

This does not mean that you only take one approach, for example, that you are purely logical and completely ignore people's feelings. Rather, your emphasis is on one approach and this is the way you naturally tend to operate.

Our society tends to value objectivity and logic in decision-making, and a decision based on how you or others feel about it is often considered weaker. Such a decision might be criticized as having "let our feelings run away with us," or "let our heart rule our head." However, it's important to incorporate both thinking and feeling elements into our decision-making and, although Jung doubted whether we could ever fully balance all of our mental functions, he was clear that the healthy path involved seeking to do this.

phobias

Most of us are afraid of something, whether spiders, heights, or dentists. Some of these are very common fears, whereas some seem particularly unusual—I had a friend who couldn't bear exposed foam rubber. Most of the time these fears don't trouble us greatly. My wife shrieks from time to time when a particularly vigorous spider visits her, but she soon recovers. However, for some people such fears have a major impact and dominate their lives.

These fears are called "phobias," after Phobos, the Greek god of fear. Phobias are generally divided into specific phobias (such as the fear of snakes or doctors) and social phobia, a more general fear of social situations. In America it is estimated that 7 percent of men and 16 percent of women will suffer from a phobia at some point in their lives.

Why Be Afraid?
Psychologists have identified different causes for phobias. Freud thought they were primitive drives that where being repressed and emerged in disguise. A fear of trains might therefore have nothing to do with trains, but actually be a terror of an old schoolteacher who was a train enthusiast.

As we've already seen, Russian physiologist Ivan Pavlov found that he could make a dog's mouth water just by ringing a bell. All he had to do was ring the bell when feeding the dog, who would then associate the bell with food. Soon the bell alone could get the dog to salivate, even when no food was presented. This "conditioning" is what some psychologists think may happen with a phobia. We have made an unconscious association between the stimulus (for instance, a spider) and the feeling of fear. Rationally we know that we don't need to be scared—those with a phobia generally recognize that their level of fear is out of proportion to what they are fearful of—but somewhere in the brain the association has been made and it is hard to break.

Even seeing someone else being afraid of something can make you start to fear it.

In theory, you could make someone afraid of anything. If you got an electric shock every time you saw a puppy you might well start breaking out in a sweat and panicking every time you met one one, a feeling that would persist even when you were no longer given a shock and you knew consciously that the puppy wouldn't harm you.

Hard-Wired to Be Scared?
The autonomic nervous system (ANS) controls the main organs and, therefore, the pulse and respiration rates, perspiration, and digestion. There is evidence that some people's ANS is more sensitive than most to being aroused. These people may seem more "edgy" or "jumpy," and they can react more strongly and quickly to any fear-provoking stimulus.

There is also evidence to suggest that all of us are predisposed to be more fearful about some things than others. There are more people who have a spider phobia than a knife phobia, car phobia, or accident phobia, yet where I live you have almost no chance of being hurt by a spider. Martin Seligman suggests that the reason we're prone to be phobic toward some things is that evolution has "prepared" our brains to be afraid of them. These "prepared" fears are mainly of dangerous creatures (spiders, snakes, insects, and so on), disease (dirt, maggots, decaying meat, and the like), and people who can be a danger to you. These were the biggest threats to us in our primitive past.

Laboratory experiments have shown that it is much quicker to condition a fear for a "prepared" stimulus than something neutral, and that it takes far longer to break the connection. For example, it's much easier to make a rhesus monkey afraid of a toy crocodile than it is to make it afraid of a toy rabbit.

Mix and Match

There seems to be an endless list of phobias. Some are common and well recognized, but for many it's simply a matter of putting a word (preferably a Greek one) in front of "phobia." Can you match the following phobias to the cause of the fear?

1. Claustrophobia	**a.** death
2. Agoraphobia	**b.** everything
3. Arachnophobia	**c.** closed spaces
4. Mycophobia	**d.** snakes
5. Necrophobia	**e.** spiders
6. Iatrophobia	**f.** being buried alive
7. Panphobia	**g.** public places
8. Ophidiophobia	**h.** doctors
9. Taphephobia	**i.** mushrooms and fungi

If you found this exercise very traumatic you might like to know that hellenologophobia is the fear of pseudo-scientific words.

Answers: 1c, 2g, 3e, 4i, 5a, 6h, 7b, 8d, 9f.

nightmares

Modern life is doubtless stressful for many people, but few of us have to deal with genuine terror except in our dreams. Most people have nightmares from time to time, so what are they and what, if anything, do they mean?

The Physiology of Dreams

As we fall asleep our mind becomes less active and the pattern of our brain waves changes, getting slower and slower. Sleep psychologists have identified that we move through four different levels of this "slow wave" sleep, each deeper than the last. However, once we have reached the deepest level, our brains become more active than when we're awake. This phase is called REM sleep (because of the rapid eye movements evident), and it's here we begin to dream.

Few of our dreams are remembered and it's generally those that are interupted when we wake that we recall. Alarm clocks, partners, or children might be the cause, but if the dream is particularly distressing then the dream itself may wake us.

Dream Content

People all around the world experience nightmares and although there are some cultural variations in detail there are consistent themes. Being chased is very common, and many people have dreamed of being naked in public, losing things, or sitting an exam that they forgot to revise for.

Some psychologists believe that dreams are just random mental noise that occurs while our brains tidy up and clean out the day's thoughts. However, throughout history dreams have been interpreted as messages and premonitions, whether from a god or from the spirit world. Two notable Biblical examples are Joseph and Daniel, who were both able to interpret dreams.

Try This: Lucid Dreaming

Lucid dreams are those in which you're aware that you are dreaming and are able to take some control of what happens. They can be hard to achieve as realizing we are dreaming often wakes us. Among psychophysiologist Stephen LaBerge's suggestions for increasing your chances of a lucid dream are:

1. Become familiar with the content of your dreams—keep a dream diary.

2. Get used to asking yourself if you're awake during the day. Do this and you'll be more likely to do it in dreams.

3. Check a clock, some writing, or an immovable object, then do it again—if it has changed or moved then you're probably dreaming.

Dreams: The Guardians of Sleep

Such religious interpretations have largely given way to psychoanalytic theories; although dreams remain the subject of much pseudoscientific speculation alongside well-founded research.

The most famous contributions in the field were made by Sigmund Freud in his 1899 book *The Interpretation of Dreams*. Freud believed that the distressing thoughts that we lock away in our unconscious can surface during the night while our mind is at rest. To stop these thoughts waking us, the content is disguised into the content we see in our dreams. For example, a man might dream of a monkey. Now different dream dictionaries tell us that a monkey symbolizes playfulness, mischief, or deceit. But if this man's estranged sister used to have a favorite toy monkey, Freud thought the monkey might represent her. Dreaming of his sister may distress and awaken him, so she is replaced with the image of a monkey in the dream.

In contrast, Seattle-born psychologist Calvin S. Hall believed that dreams are there to reveal messages rather than hide them. He stated that they are "letters to yourself" giving you different perspectives on your life.

Another take on dreams is offered by Finnish psychologist Antti Revonsuo of the Center for Cognitive Neuroscience at the University of Turku. He suggests that dreams are there to help us practice dealing with threats in a safe environment, so nightmares serve a useful training function.

Night Terrors

Night terror (*pavor nocturnus*) is where a person, most typically a child between the ages of two and six years, wakes in great distress and confusion. It differs from a nightmare in that there is no dream to relate the fear to, just an incredibly strong emotion. Unlike dreams, the night terrors occur outside of REM sleep. Although they are most prevalent in children, adults can experience night terrors and regular incidences can be very distressing.

the politics of fear

Psychology has long been used as a tool of war. Propaganda can embolden and unite allies or demoralize foes. Misinformation can create confusion and division whilst in recent years even loud and abrasive music has been used to undermine the morale of opposition forces. However, throughout history fear and terror have been the most constant themes.

Fear on the Battlefield

Historically, battles are not always won by the side that kills more of their enemy, but by the one that stays on the field. Armies retreat or rout because they are fearful or demoralized, because soldiers believe they will not survive.

For centuries soldiers wore tall hats and broad epaulettes to make them look bigger, just as a mammal preparing for combat will make its hair stand on end. War cries, the skirl of the bagpipes, the beating of drums and shields can have the same effect as a lion's roar or the howling of a cat.

Terror, carefully deployed, may even remove the need for battle. The Mongols who conquered much of Europe and Asia from the 13th century onwards were masters of this strategy. They would slaughter those who refused to submit to them, then send messengers on to the next town to warn the locals that the terrible Mongols were approaching. Tales of what happened to the last town that had resisted would be circulated and peace envoys would be sent out.

Unexpected Terror

Laboratory experiments show that if you can anticipate an unpleasant stimulus you tend to cope with it better. A light that warns that a shock is coming enables rats to cope better with the ensuing trauma, perhaps because they can relax better when the light is not on as they know no shock is coming.

Terrorist attacks capitalize on the reverse of this phenomenon: no one knows when an attack will come and everyone is a potential target. High states of readiness are tiring and stressful, but there is no point at which you can be reassured that there will not be an attack.

Often the fear of a weapon outweighs its ability to inflict physical harm, and rockets are a classic example of this. In the early 19th century, Britain was one of the first European states to employ rockets on the battlefield. As they spiralled madly, screaming in flight, enemy soldiers waited to see if the unpredictable missiles would head toward them. Casualties were thought to be few, but the terror they inspired was considered highly useful.

Terror tactics have also found uses away from the battlefield. One of the most famous example was *la Terreur*, the name given to the period in the French Revolution from September 1793 to July 1794 when the warring parties within the newly formed revolutionary government sought to retain power in a chaotic and violent state. Under Maximillian Robespierre, they used execution by the guillotine to subjegate a frightened population. Much of this fear arose from the uncertainty about who the next victim might be; in the ever-changing political landscape one day's favored son of the revolution could, the next day, be denounced as the state's mortal enemy. Almost inevitably, this reign of terror ended when Robespierre himself fell victim to the guillotine.

The Terror of Dracula

Vlad III of Wallachia, better know to the world as Dracula, or Vlad the Impaler, was one of the medieval world's greatest exponents of the politics of terror. As ruler of Wallachia, between Hungary and the invading Ottoman Turks, he struck fear into the hearts of his own population and invading armies alike.

He is best known for his practice of impaling his enemies on wooden stakes on which it would take them days to die. When Sultan Mehmed II moved a huge army into Wallachia to bring Dracula to heel, he was confronted with the sight of 20,000 Turkish prisoners impaled on stakes. Despite being a seasoned warrior it is said he turned round and headed straight back to Constantinople and that he would never again sleep in the dark.

The name of Dracula is now associated with horror stories, but in his native Romania he remains a national hero.

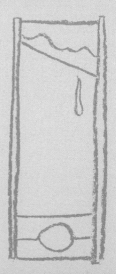

the cost of fearlessness

It has not been uncommon when administering personality questionnaires to my clients to find people with very high levels of stress and anxiety. They often report that their lives are uncomfortable and they wish that they did not feel things as keenly as they do. But although it may make their lives harder, their fearfulness does have some benefits. What would life be like if we really were fearless?

Fear as a Warning

The most obvious answer is that a life without fear would be a short one. The person who doesn't learn about the dangers of heights, fire, and fast-moving cars may not survive very long. Simply *knowing* these things might not be enough: we cannot attend to everything all the time, so our fear responses help us focus.

Beyond this we have already seen how fear prepares our bodies for dangerous situations. Our fight, flight, or freeze mechanism kicks in when we need it and helps us deal with physical threats. This may seem less relevant in the 21st century, but most performers and sports people will tell you that if they're too calm and relaxed then they can't turn in a top performance. We need the adrenaline to operate at our best.

Social Benefits of Fear

Imagine yourself in the trenches, about to go and fight for the first time. You're scared of dying and maybe just as scared that you will panic and fail your comrades. Your experienced sergeant turns to you and asks, "Scared?" Sheepishly you nod and reply, "You too?" He smiles and replies "Nah … not me. I'm no coward."

That's not a comforting reply. We might like brave colleagues in a situation like this, but we like it more when they admit they too are nervous. It validates our own feelings and we can judge ourselves less harshly.

Those people who are overconfident can often seem unapproachable. If they have not experienced weakness themselves they may be less able to understand or tolerate it in others, which can make them very unsympathetic colleagues. Fear is part of the human condition and it is hard to relate to those who don't feel it.

The Danger of the Fearless

One of the defining features of sociopaths (more popularly known as psychopaths) is that they don't seem to feel anxiety in the same way as other people. Because they seem less able to develop a fear response to negative stimuli, such as punishments, they tend to act impetuously and without regard for the outcome. When you add this to a failure to empathize with other human beings, to appreciate or care about their suffering, it is clear why sociopaths can pose such a danger.

The Pratfall Effect

Those clients of mine didn't want their own fear, but equally they didn't want to be the type of people whose fearlessness they envied. We generally like to see that a person has a few flaws and uncertainties. Social psychologist Elliot Aronson notes that when the seemingly godlike President Kennedy made his biggest political blunder, in the Bay of Pigs fiasco, his popularity actually increased.

Fascinatingly, Aronson was able to recreate the effect in the laboratory. People were played tapes of four characters, all played by the same actor. Two of these were of superior ability and two of average ability, and one of each type had made a blunder. The person of superior ability who made a blunder was rated as most attractive. Aronson dubbed this the "pratfall effect."

The Thrill of Fear

Most people enjoy the thrill of fear to some extent, whether it be a horror film, a roller-coaster ride, or engaging in a physical sport. Some people seem to need the excitement that comes with taking risks. Psychologist Martin Zuckerman has identified a "sensation-seeking" personality trait that can assess whether people are more or less prone to risk-taking. Rate the following statements as true or false:

1. I like being around unpredictable people.

2. I'm rarely bored.

3. I like being places I've never been before.

4. Home is where I'm happiest.

5. I enjoy very physical sports.

6. I'd rather be with people I know well than with strangers.

Author's Comments

If more of statements 1, 3, and 5 than 2, 4, and 6 are true for you, you may be the type of person who enjoys the excitement of being in physically or socially risky situations.

fear of god

Throughout most of human history we've had little understanding of the enormous forces of nature that affect our lives. Even today many lives are dependent upon whether rain comes, a volcano erupts, or diseases break out. We know that a major component of psychological fear is the amount of control we have, and primitive peoples felt even less in control of these forces that governed their lives than we seem to be now. If you believe that it is a god that controls these forces, who has the power of life and death over you and over whom you have no power, then fearing him, her, or it seems like rather a wise move.

More modern Western monotheistic perspectives are dominated by the idea that God is meant to be good and faithful, but how much more fearful would you be if this were not the case?

The Greek gods were certainly worth fearing. Immortal and immensely powerful as they were, they still retained all the faults of humans including pettiness, selfishness, and spite combined with very creative ideas on punishment. Some were even defined by their faults, such as Eris, the goddess of strife and discord. It was Eris who initiated the situation in which Paris had to choose which of three goddesses, Hera, Athena or Aphrodite, was the most beautiful. Given that sort of choice,

you know the day will end badly, with two very angry goddesses, and in this instance it sparked the Trojan wars.

These pantheons of imperfect gods inevitably meant trouble for the poor mortals who spent a great deal of time and effort trying to appease them. But when it comes to monotheism, why would we fear a loving God who had our interests at heart? The phrase "The fear of the Lord is the beginning of wisdom" is taken from Psalm 110 and Proverbs 9, texts that are important to all the Abrahamic religions: Judaism, Christianity, and Islam. This is not an isolated statement. The Old Testament, which is, to varying degrees, important to all three religions, has 103 references to fearing God, and the Christian New Testament and Muslim Koran add more.

The word "fearing" is interpreted in some cases as showing appropriate respect and deference to God, but it's often translated from words which do indicate real fear, dread, and terror. Why should we feel this?

One answer is that it simply shows that a believer has an appreciation of just what an awesome concept God is. No matter how friendly an all-powerful being is, the sheer size and power of it would naturally instill fear. When angels, the messengers of God, appear in the Bible, the first thing they normally say is "Do not be afraid"; the implication being that the presence of angels induces fear, not necessarily because they are unexpected but because of their their power and purity. We often associate goodness with meekness, mildness, and being non-threatening, perhaps even with weakness.

C. S. Lewis addressed this in his novel *The Lion, the Witch and the Wardrobe*, which is a Christian allegory. When the children hear about Aslan, the lion who is the rightful and benevolent ruler of Narnia, they ask if he is safe. They are assured he is not; he is good but not "safe."

Another reason for fear is that the Abrahamic religions teach that God is just, and an honest judge will not turn a blind eye to wrongdoing. However, they also state that he is merciful, which in theological terms is often contrary to justice—justice demands an appropriate punishment for wrongdoing, mercy overrides this—but one cannot presume upon mercy.

A Shared Fear

Christianity, Islam, and Judaism share many roots, all recognizing Abraham as a fundamental figure in God's plan for the world—hence the term "Abrahamic religions."

The theologies of the three religions differ dramatically in many respects, but they all make reference to the wisdom of fearing God. In the Jewish Torah we read "...fear your God. For I am your Lord." In the Christian scriptures St. Peter says, "I now realize how true it is that God does not show favoritism but accepts men from every nation who fear him and do what is right." In Islam's Surah 26 we find, "So fear Allah and obey me."

Although various religions differ in the way that atonement has to be made or forgiveness sought and accepted, displeasing or alienating yourself from the source of all life and power would have to be an act of questionable wisdom.

Chapter 8

emotions with attitude

guilt: costs and benefits

Although guilt is a universal emotion, it's not one of the basic emotions that occur automatically from a very early age. Rather, it's a social emotion, and it's hard to feel guilty until you can appreciate other people's feelings.

Evolutionary psychologists believe that guilt developed to ensure that people could work together. In increasingly complex and co-operative environments, you need to know whether the people you're relying on can be trusted. If people transparently suffer guilt when they do something wrong, they're much better to work with than those who can cheat you and keep a poker face.

Even if guilt is developed socially, we don't need other people around to feel guilty. Freud believed that we learn what is right and wrong early on, the rules and punishments being handed out by others. But as we develop we learn to monitor ourselves, and warn ourselves about the outcome of wrongdoing. The part of the personality that does this, the super-ego, is concerned not only with wrongs to others but generalizes these to any of our failings. Our guilt is therefore inherent and we can carry it around with us even if there is nobody else around to make us feel guilty.

Guilt and Religion

Because guilt can be framed as a moral emotion, it is often characterized as being an important facet of religion. Wrongdoing cannot be hidden from the theistic God—who, being omniscient, tends to remember things. Yet theistic religions such as Judaism, Islam, and Christianity can present guilt as a positive element of a relationship with God—believers often perceive that the process of recognizing and acknowledging wrongdoing enables them to move beyond it.

Religion is often caricatured as promoting an unhealthy level of guilt, yet according to Freud we will always have guilt with us. Religion and spirituality can offer one way of dealing with this guilt and resolving it. Theistic religions generally have procedures for making amends, usually by some form of confession and often by acts of absolution, thus ending the feelings of guilt.

Guilt or Shame?

The terms "guilt" and "shame" are often used interchangeably and various definitions have been suggested. The most common distinction in psychology is that guilt relates to a negative behavior, something that you've done wrong. Shame, on the other hand, relates to a negative aspect of yourself. I'm guilty about what I did or thought, but feel shame for who I am or what I am.

Guilt-Proneness

Some people seem more prone to a sense of guilt than others, regardless of whether they have done anything wrong. They worry about things they did or didn't do, things they should or shouldn't have said. See whether the following statements are true or false for you:

1. I feel slightly uncomfortable around police officers or security guards, even though I have done nothing wrong.

2. I rarely worry about other people's opinions of me.

3. If my boss asks to speak to me my first thought is that I must have done something wrong.

4. If your best effort is not good enough you just have to accept it.

5. I sometimes find myself apologizing too much over very trivial matters.

6. You're always going to upset some people as you go through life so there is no point worrying about it.

Author's Comments

If you found items 1, 3, and 5 more true for you than you did 2, 4, and 6 this may suggest you are guilt prone, tend to judge yourself harshly, and assume you've done things wrong. It doesn't necessarily infer that you have anything to feel guilty about. In fact, the opposite may apply; those who are more prone to feeling guilty may be less likely to do things that will make them feel guilty.

Have You Ever Seen a Guilty Cat?

Social emotions need social contexts to develop in, and it's only species that have social hierarchies that tend to demonstrate guilt. Dogs are naturally pack animals with strict hierarchies. Ask dog owner if they've ever seen their dogs looking guilty when they've

done something wrong and they will probably be able to furnish you with several examples. Now ask cat owners the same question and they'll probably laugh at the absurdity of the idea. Cats are, by nature, more independent creatures.

ataraxia

Many philosophies and religions direct their followers toward a state of inner calm and peace. This has taken many names and forms throughout history but is characterized by a freedom from worry and detachment from the outside world, an absence of passion, and perhaps a transcendent experience, lucidity, and a deeper understanding of reality.

For some, such as the ancient Greek Epicureans who called it *ataraxia*, achieving this state is the goal to life, as it is the highest form of happiness. For Buddhists, Nirvana is a state that one seeks to achieve, where all craving and preoccupations are gone and the person is at peace with the world. In other belief systems, such as Christian mysticism, such a state is considered helpful in coming closer to God but is not an end in itself.

Meditation

Many faiths and belief systems encourage the use of meditation as a way of achieving this desired state, or training the self to transcend to higher spiritual levels. Though it is often associated with Eastern belief systems, such as Buddhism and Hinduism, most religions have a mystical tradition that emphasizes this practice.

There are two main approaches to meditation: "open mediation" involves trying to empty the mind of all thought; whereas "concentrative meditation" focuses the mind on one thing to the exclusion of all else. Most spiritual approaches to meditation take the latter course. In Christian mysticism a person might focus on one verse in the Bible, a facet of God's love, or a simple phrase like "Kyrie eleison," which means "Lord have Mercy." In other systems, such as transcendental meditation, a sound (called a mantra) is used.

Both forms are thought to help in achieving a state of calm and altered consciousness, and claims that meditiation causes any harm are rare. However, some approaches claim to bring more than just calm, such as a greater awareness of God or the universe.

The Science of Meditation

There has been a great deal published on the psychological and physiological impact of meditation, though the research is recognized to be variable in quality. However, some studies report that brain waves change during meditation from the beta waves we see when a person is active and awake to the much slower alpha and theta waves that we see when a person is very relaxed, calm, or on the borders of sleep. There have also been many studies examining the ability of those experienced in meditation to stay in this state despite interruptions and attempts to disturb them.

David S. Holmes is a psychologist who brought together the available literature and studies on the topic and concluded on the basis of the mixed reports and findings that there is no real difference between meditation and simply having a rest. He found that meditation did enhance feelings of calm and it affected thoughts and feelings, but that these changes were no different from just spending a while sitting down and doing (and thinking about) nothing. There were no differences in brain patterns or other physiological or psychological phenomena between meditation and resting.

His results are controversial and it is not surprising that they have been challenged by many of those who practice and believe in meditation. However, data to the contrary is not strong enough to undermine his basic position—though clearly physiological results offer little in the way of an evaluation of any claimed spiritual benefits that may or may not occur.

Do-It-Yourself Meditation

Many religions teach that specific words, prayers, or practices need to be employed in pursuit of meditation, but secular forms do exist. These are often based on the work of American cardiologist Herbert Benson who has done much to promote a standard secular approach to mediation:

1. Get yourself into a quiet space where you will not be disturbed.

2. Sit still with your eyes closed and your muscles relaxed.

3. You should pick a word to say that you will repeat throughout the session. This might be a holy word or prayer for some people, but in secular mediation the word "one" is often recommended.

4. Now observe your breathing and focus on it. Don't try to change it, just attend as you breathe in and out. When you breathe out, say your chosen word in your head.

5. Continue this for 10–20 minutes. If you get distracted by other thoughts, don't worry, just send them away and return to your counting and breathing.

6. When you have finished, sit still for a couple of minutes before returning to your normal routine.

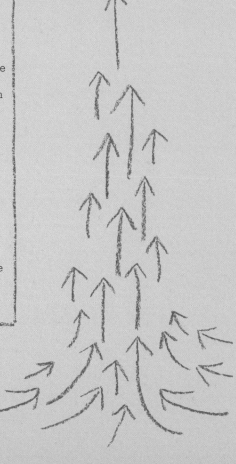

the power of hatred

There seems to be a broad consensus that hatred is a negative and destructive emotion, so why do so many otherwise decent and kind people nurture deep-seated hatred toward other individuals or groups?

Prejudice

Prejudice appears to develop fairly easily. It usually starts with a stereotype—a generalization about a group concerning some facet that makes them distinctive. The stereotype is usually based on limited information and exposure, or on contact with an atypical subset. For example, people visiting London might reasonably think Londoners are always in a hurry, because they mainly see Londoners when they're rushing to or from work, not when they're at home. From that point the stereotype becomes self-maintaining. If you hear about a Londoner in a rush it strengthens the stereotype; if you hear about one who isn't, then you might think "that's not like a Londoner." Individual instances are unlikely to modify your stereotype; so it develops and maintains itself.

This may sound harmless, but stereotypes invariably have a negative aspect, and so prejudice sets in. You've now defined a set of people as "different" from you. And if, for example, you find yourself competing for jobs with Londoners, they become "those people who can't be bothered to make any time for me." They become perceived as a threat and a convenient group to blame and direct your frustrations against. This is exacerbated if those around you hold similar views. In times of difficulty this distance between you and the "other" group can turn to contempt and hatred.

History and psychological research have both shown how these stereotypes and prejudices have developed against all manner of groups, especially those defined by race, gender, religion, nationality, sexual orientation, and disability.

Cognitive Dissonance

There may have been a time when you found yourself doing something unkind and you may have thought "I really am a rat." But this impression doesn't generally last long. It often changes to "He's the rat, he deserved that" or "I'm sure she doesn't really mind."

It was in the 1950s that the American social psychologist Leon Festinger first proposed the idea of "cognitive dissonance" to explain this phenomenon. The theory states that people don't like holding contrary thoughts such as "I'm a good person" and "I did something horrible." They'll generally change one of these thoughts or "cognitions" or create a third cognition that reconciles the two, such as: "but I didn't realize at the time that what I was doing was wrong."

The cognition that is most resistant to change is the self-image, so people who think they're decent—which is (unsurprisingly) most of us—will generally end up feeling that what they did was consistent with being a good person. A racist can generally think "I'm a good person," in spite of having been nasty to a person of a different race, by bridging it with a thought such as "but they don't have the same feelings as me."

As a general rule we might expect that the more you dislike someone, the worse you'll behave toward them. Perversely, cognitive dissonance suggests that the worse you treat someone, the more you'll dislike them. This is because you need to justify why you acted so badly to them; and the more unpleasant you decide they are, the more they deserved it. You tell yourself you're not a bad person for being unpleasant to them, they're just getting what they deserve.

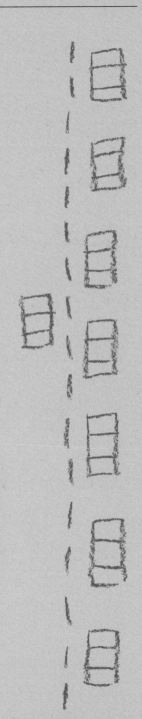

Inside-Laners—Prejudice in Action

One time, when driving to an unfamiliar destination, I was late and getting increasingly stressed. I needed to pull into the inside lane of traffic; however, despite repeated attempts, not one of the people in the inside lane would let me in. I was getting increasingly irate at the injustice of it all when I saw a road sign indicating that I didn't need to change lane.

Just then someone from the inside lane signaled to pull out into my lane. It only lasted for a fraction of a second, but the thought flashed through my head "I'm not going to let an Inside-Laner out, none of them let me in."

What a ridiculous idea. People on the inside lane were not any kind of group, and that particular "Inside-Laner" had absolutely no link with those who had refused me a favor. Yet for a split second I was able to hold her accountable for what, in my stressed state, I held their crimes to be. And yes, I did let her out.

pride: the great barrier

"Pride goes before destruction; a haughty spirit before a fall." (Proverbs 16:18)

Emotions are normally identified as being either positive or negative, but pride is strangely divided. Psychologically, self-esteem is recognized as fundamental to mental health, yet too much pride in oneself can be extremely damaging both psychologically and socially, as well as being considered one of the greatest personality flaws.

From an evolutionary perspective pride is taken to signal the opposite of weakness. It asserts that a person is important and makes a claim for a high place in the hierarchy. Consider the physical expression of pride—it's all about making you appear bigger: puffing out the chest, perhaps with hands on hips, lifting the chin, and pulling the head back. The posture appears to be recognized universally and is the standard on military parade grounds around the world—it is a strong stance.

The Problem with Pride

Pride can have positive connotations. We talk about "taking a pride" in what we do, and terms such as "black pride" or "gay pride" are about reasserting a sense of esteem in the wake of historical oppression and denigration. An excess of pride, however, can be extremely damaging. If a person is too proud to seek help, accept advice, listen to others, or apologize, it can have a devastating impact not only on social relationships but also on the ability to make sound decisions.

Theologically, pride is often considered offensive because it is seen as an individual placing him- or herself above their proper station. In some Christian traditions pride is considered the worst of the Seven Deadly Sins, on the basis that a proud person not only places him- or herself above others, but also because such a person implicitly denies reliance on God.

Pride is also considered a problem in the teachings of non-theistic religions, such as Buddhism, because it encourages too much reliance on self, triggers disrespect, and is a delusion that is a barrier to enlightenment.

Although pride is a universal emotion, the values associated with it vary culturally. In hierarchical cultures, such as traditional Japanese and English societies, humility is valued highly, and self-aggrandizement is considered less acceptable than in many less rigidly structured societies.

The Two Prides

Jessica Tracy and Rick Robins have identified two separate types of pride. Hubris, elsewhere called alpha-pride, is a pride in self; authentic pride, or beta-pride, is the pride taken in an achievement. Authentic pride tends to relate to specific skills in specific situations; it says "I did well at this test because I tried hard." Hubris is more about general underlying ability and says "I did well because I'm great."

Studies have shown that people with high levels of authentic pride tend to be more agreeable and open to others, and are more conscientious and emotionally stable. They also appear to be more outgoing and have better levels of self-esteem. Those with high levels of hubris, however, tend to be less agreeable and conscientious.

Narcissus

Personality disorders are unusual and unhelpful patterns of behavior that are persistent and inflexible. Those with narcissistic personality disorder see themselves as exceptional and unique, with uncommon ability. They will readily use others as they feel their superiority warrants, and they can be arrogant and lacking in empathy. They will always want to be the center of attention and expect to be praised and admired by those whom they see as being less important than themselves.

Unsurprisingly, those with high levels of hubristic pride are associated with narcissistic tendencies.

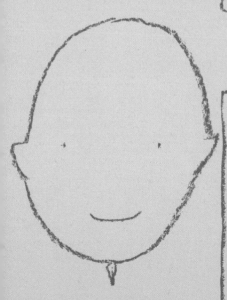

Hubris and Nemesis

Hubris is generally used to refer to a particular type of exaggerated pride that goes before a fall. It has the connotation of tempting fate with arrogance and is typified by those who become overconfident on the basis of their success. The word has ancient Greek roots, and it is also from the ancient Greeks that we take the word "nemesis"—from the Greek goddess of that name, who traditionally punished those who succumbed to hubris.

hedonism and the pursuit of pleasure

There have always been those who have made the pursuit of pleasure their focus in life. This has an obvious appeal, but deciding exactly what pleasure is and how to pursue it is a more complex issue.

Two major distinctions exist here: Is your concern with maximizing your own pleasure or everyone's? And are you concerned with basic physical gratification or some higher ideal of what pleasure is?

We can begin with Aristippus of Cyrene (c. 435–356 BCE), who typifies the quest for personal physical pleasure. Initially a follower of the great Socrates, Aristippus became an advocate, and model, of basic physical gratification. Disdaining traditional morals and caring little for what others thought of him, he believed not only that you should satisfy your personal desires but that you should not delay gratifying them.

This might appeal to some, but it is a hard practice to live. Aristippus was thought fickle and callous by his peers, and to survive such an existence you have to care neither for the opinions of others nor the demands of your own conscience. Although he did believe that you should always be in control of your appetites, rather than a slave to them, this may be hard to achieve.

In contrast, Epicurus (341–270 BCE) sought more modest pleasures, avoiding excesses of food and sex in favor of a tranquil existence. His followers withdrew from public life to enjoy contemplation and friendship. This seems like a higher moral path, and although the emphasis was on the individual's pleasure, it was stressed that one should aim not to harm others.

Epicureans saw learning and civilization as distractions that tempt humanity to achieve, thus producing ever more desires that can't be satisfied. For them, the main benefits of knowledge were that it can stop you fearing the gods (who they thought were uninterested in humanity) and death. This simple life meant controlling desire but surrendering much in the

The Utility Monster

Utilitarianism states that you should do that which maximizes pleasure and minimizes pain. This has been the foundation of many economic models for the allocation of resources. However, challenging this approach, the American philosopher Robert Nozick proposed we consider the "utility monster."

Suppose there was a monster that gained a hundred times the amount of pleasure from each unit of resource as you did. The "right" thing to do, under utilitarianism, would be to allow the utility monster to have all the resources and have none yourself.

way of achievement and service to others. Modern philosophy has presented similar perspectives. The British philosopher Jeremy Bentham (1748–1832), whose preserved body still occasionally attends meetings of University College London's college council, is credited with the idea of utilitarianism. Like Epicureanism, utilitarianism identifies the main goal of life as maximizing pleasure and minimizing pain. For Bentham, this meant considering both the duration and the intensity of the pleasure and pain, and he was content for these pleasures to be basic and physical. John Stuart Mill, who was brought up with utilitarian values, proposed instead that there were higher and lower pleasures. The former consisted of intellectual pursuits, spiritual development, and culture, the latter of physical appetites that would satisfy only briefly.

These different positions all hold to the basic premiss that life is, in the end, about pleasure, and the "goodness" of an action depends on this. Much of utilitarianism is about the greater social good rather than purely seeking what suits you best.

What Do You Really Want?

It may seem obvious to state that people want to maximize pleasure and minimize pain, but is this really enough?

Imagine one option in achieving maximum pleasure and minimum pain. This might involve being left on a surgical bed, perhaps semi-conscious, with chemicals being pumped into your brain. Perhaps there would be some surgical manipulation of the brain's pleasure centers (such as the nucleus accumbens) and much stimulation of neurotransmitter and hormone receptors. We would have to overcome the brain's tendency to adapt to stimuli and so maintain the level of pleasure and fend off pain, but is this a vision of a pleasurable future?

Would you really sacrifice the potential to achieve anything, to have any impact, enjoy relationships, and see the people you love—all for the promise of pleasure without pain?

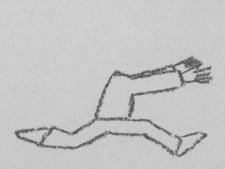

the death of compassion

Although people differ in the level of sympathy, shame, and guilt that they experience, there are always those who are quite prepared to do unpleasant things to others. Even so, most of us find it hard to imagine how people could involve themselves in the atrocities that have taken place throughout history.

In the Holocaust of the Second World War millions of Jews and other people considered "undesirable" by the Nazi state were systematically murdered on an industrial scale. As recently as 1994 the Rwanda genocide saw almost a fifth of the country's population brutally murdered by former neighbors. Even today accusations of genocide persist around the world.

But how can such horrors occur? Two of the most famous pieces of psychological research can give us some insight into how people can overcome their natural levels of compassion.

Compliance

As social creatures, we generally want to fit in. We also live in hierarchies that give us guidance on what is and isn't acceptable. When in doubt we look to our peers and authority figures to give us a lead.

In 1963 psychologist Stanley Milgram recruited people to help in what they believed was an experiment on learning. As another volunteer (actually a stooge) was put in a chair and had electrodes attached, an experimenter explained that every time this person got a question wrong the volunteer had to administer an electric shock, to see its effect on learning. After a few correct answers a wrong one was

given; the volunteer flicked the switch labeled "15 volts" and heard the sound of the other person receiving the shock.

Would you flick that switch? You might think not, but if it was a scientific study in a prestigious university (Yale) and a stern scientist is asking you … well, it must be alright.

However, with each wrong answer a higher-voltage switch is used. At 75 volts the volunteer will hear the other person moaning, at 180 volts he's asking to be let out, and soon he's banging on the walls while the volunteer is asked to administer shocks using the switches that are labeled "Danger."

I'm sure you feel absolutely certain that you would never go this far—in fact, almost 100 percent of people say they wouldn't—but 65 percent of the people taking part in the experiment did, albeit with encouragement from the experimenter. Not sick people or bad people, just normal people who told themselves it was alright because the authorities were endorsing it. It wasn't that they didn't feel compassion, many were very distressed, but they did it anyway. The experiment has been repeated many times since, in many different countries, and the results tend to be the same.

The Prison Experiment
In another famous study, psychologist Philip
Zimbardo recruited students at the prestigious
Stanford University. He randomly split them into
two groups: one of prison guards and one of
prisoners. They were then taken for a two-week
stay in a mock prison in the basement of the
university.

After just six days the experiment had to be
abandoned. The guards were treating the
prisoners like animals, enjoying being cruel
to them, while the prisoners became "servile
and dehumanized." Zimbardo noted how "in
less than a week the experience … undid
(temporarily) a lifetime of learning … and the
ugliest, most base, pathological side of human
nature surfaced."

Remember, these two groups of people
were exactly the same; the prisoners hadn't
done anything wrong, neither group was
smarter, stronger, kinder, or better in any way
than the other. Simply putting them into this
environment and these roles changed the way
they thought about, and acted toward, other
human beings.

Clearly, Milgram's and Zimbardo's experiments
on their own are not enough to explain how
something like the Holocaust can happen, but
they do show how we can override our feelings
of compassion and carry out acts that, from a
safe distance, we would usually abhor. If we
combine this with the cognitive dissonance
discussed on the previous pages, which helps
justify our acts, and the stereotyping that
dehumanizes our victims, we can see how
some of the building blocks are in place for
committing acts our emotions and conscience
would not normally sanction.

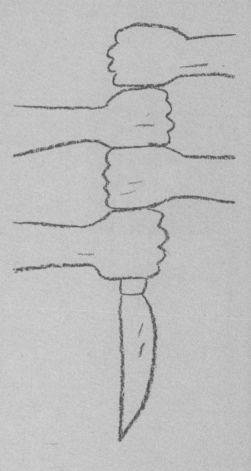

viktor e. frankl

Born in Vienna in 1905, Viktor Emil Frankl chose medicine as a career and became a successful psychiatrist and neurologist. However, being Jewish, his opportunities were restricted after the Nazis took control of Austria, and in 1942 he was sent to the concentration camps.

Life in the Death Camps

Frankl described the emotional life of those interned in the death camps. First came shock, then a terrible despair and apathy. With too little food and sleep, many people became irritable and lost interest in everything but surviving the moment. Some have described it as retreating to a more primitive state, though Frankl notes that many people retained an interest in politics, religion, and food.

Just as one must ask how people could commit the terrible atrocities of the Holocaust, the question also arises of how the victims coped—not only with the impact of being in the death camps, but in the world afterwards. Viktor Frankl was a Holocaust survivor who spent three and a half years in concentration camps, losing his wife, brother, and parents to them. He not only survived but went on to provide hope and meaning for many.

Logotherapy

Frankl was the creator of "logotherapy" (from the Greek *logos*; "meaning"). It is known as the third school of Viennese psychotherapy after Freud's and Adler's.

Logotherapy focuses on helping patients find meaning in their lives and uses a range of interesting techniques. The best known is "paradoxical intention," in which you do the opposite of what you want to achieve. For example, if you are having trouble sleeping, but want to get a good night's sleep, you would aim to stay awake as long as you can. Having changed your focus, you should lose your fear of sleeplessness, and so sleep becomes more likely.

Frankl felt that despair was not inevitable, even in such an awful situation. He noticed there were still some who looked after the needs of comrades and who proved that "Everything can be taken from a man but one thing: the last of the human freedoms— to choose one's attitude in any given set of circumstances, to choose one's own way..." (*Man's Search for Meaning*, 1956.)

Frankl chose to find meaning in the midst of suffering. He focused on helping others and resolved to laugh and make at least one joke a day.

The Doctor of the Soul

Upon his liberation from the camps, Frankl saw that the suffering was not over. Many of those who were freed became numb, bitter, and disillusioned. In his approach to these people Frankl departed dramatically from his great Viennese forebear, Sigmund Freud, in his thinking. Where, for Freud, the human was very much a biological system driven by primitive urges, Frankl saw us as transcendent and spiritual beings who can rise above their environment.

Frankl saw that the basic problem for humans was an "existential crisis"—people didn't know what they were for. He rejected aims such as seeking pleasure, material gain, fame, and power; arguing that these are just by-products of some people's journey, but will not satisfy in themselves.

Freedom and Responsibility

If we're not purely products of our biology or environment and really are free to choose our own path, this also means that we are ultimately responsible for our choices. Frankl said that there were only two types of people, "decent men and indecent men," and he could find both types in the victims of the camp but also in the guards. You are free to be either, but you are responsible for what you are. To this end, Frankl suggested that the Statue of Liberty on the east coast of America should be complemented by a Statue of Responsibility on the west.

> ## Finding Meaning
>
> Meaning does not have to be a great life quest. Rather it differs from person to person, from day to day.
>
> Frankl said there were three ways to find meaning. One is to do a deed; to be active and involved in your projects. Another is to experience something or encounter someone; this could be appreciating beauty or falling in love. Then there is your attitude to life, to events, and finally to your own suffering. It isn't what happens to you that matters so much, it's your attitude to it.

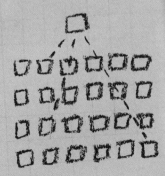

index of philosophers and psychologists

Ainsworth, Mary
Dates: 1913–1999
Nationality: American
Related Areas:
Developmental psychology
Related Entries:
"The strange situation"
on p. 69

Aristippus of Cyrene
Dates: c.465–356 BCE
Nationality: Greek
Related Areas:
The philosophy of the
pursuit of pleasure
Related Entries:
Hedonism and the pursuit of
pleasure on p. 144

Aristotle
Dates: 384–322 BCE
Nationality: Greek
Related Areas:
A broad range of
philosophical subjects
including metaphysics,
logic, and ethics
Related Entries:
The role of anger on p. 144

Bandura, Albert
Dates: b.1925
Nationality: Canadian
Related Areas:
Social cognitive theory
and self-efficacy
Related Entries:
The "Bobo" doll studies
on p. 85

Bard, Philip
Dates: 1898-1977
Nationality: American
Related Areas:
The functions of the nervous
system, especially the brain's
involvement in emotions
Related Entries:
The Cannon–Bard theory
on p. 51

Beck, Aaron
Dates: b.1921
Nationality: American
Related Areas:
Depression and cognitive
behavioral therapy
Related Entries:
Depressive cognitions
on p. 104

Benson, Herbert
Dates: b. 1935
Nationality: American
Related Areas:
Meditation and the
relaxation response.
Related Entries:
Secular meditation on p. 137

Bentham, Jeremy
Dates: 1748–1832
Nationality: English
Related Areas:
Utilitarianism and the pursuit
of the greatest happiness
Related Entries:
Hedonism and the pursuit of
pleasure on p. 145

Bini, Lucio
Dates: 1908–1964
Nationality: Italian
Related Areas:
The development of electro-
convulsive therapy
Related Entries:
Electro-convulsive therapy
on p. 145

Bowlby, John
Dates: 1907–1990
Nationality: British
Related Areas:
Child development and
attachment theory
Related Entries:
Attachment theory
on p. 68

Cannon, Walter
Dates: 1871–1945
Nationality: American
Related Areas:
The bodily effects of
emotional excitement
Related Entries:
The Cannon–Bard theory
on p. 51

**Csikszentmihalyi,
Mihaly**
Dates: b. 1934
Nationality: Hungarian
Related Areas:
Positive psychology
Related Entries:
The theory of flow on p. 112

Darwin, Charles (naturalist)
Dates: 1809–1882
Nationality: British
Related Areas:
Evolution and natural
selection; the evolution of
emotions
Related Entries:
The evolution of emotions on
pp. 20–1

Descartes, René
Dates: 1596–1650
Nationality: French
Related Areas:
Metaphysics and
epistemology.
Related Entries:
The "Method of Doubt"
on p. 26

Diener, Ed
Dates: b. 1946
Nationality: American
Related Areas:
The psychology of well-being
Related Entries:
The measurement of
happiness on p. 101

Dollard, John
Dates: 1900–1980
Nationality: American
Related Areas:
Theories of aggressive
behavior
Related Entries:
The frustration–aggression
hypothesis on p. 84

Ekman, Paul
Dates: b. 1934
Nationality: American
Related Areas:
The study of emotions in
relation to facial expressions
Related Entries:
The universality of
emotional expressions
on pp. 31, 36, 38–9

Epicurus
Dates: 341–270 BCE
Nationality: Greek
Related Areas:
The Epicurean school
of philosophy
Related Entries:
The pursuit of happiness
on p. 144

Festinger, Leon
Dates: 1919–1989
Nationality: American
Related Areas:
Social psychology
Related Entries:
The theory of cognitive
dissonance on p. 144

Fisher, Helen (anthropologist)
Dates: b. 1945
Nationality: American
Related Areas:
The biology of love
and attraction
Related Entries:
The emotional stages of love
on p. 64

Frankl, Viktor E.
Dates: 1905–1997
Nationality: Austrian
Related Areas:
Neurology and psychiatry
Related Entries:
The foundation of logotherapy
on pp. 148–9

Freud, Sigmund
Dates: 1856–1939
Nationality: Austrian
Related Areas:
Theories of the unconscious
mind and the interpretation
of dreams
Related Entries:
The foundation of
psychoanalysis on pp. 72–3

Gilbert, Daniel
Dates: b. 1957
Nationality: American
Related Areas:
Social psychology and
affective forecasting
Related Entries:
The concept of miswanting
on p. 59

Gottman, John
Dates: b. 1942
Nationality: American
Related Areas:
The analysis of relationships
and marriage
Related Entries:
The likelihood of marital
breakup on on p. 74

Hall, Calvin
Dates: 1909–1985
Nationality: American
Related Areas:
The study of temperament and behavior, as well as dream content
Related Entries:
The study of dream content on p. 126

Hippocrates
Dates: c. 460–370 BCE
Nationality: Greek
Related Areas:
Medicine
Related Entries:
The study of mental illness on p. 20

James, William
Dates: 1842–1910
Nationality: American
Related Areas:
The relationship between stimuli and emotions; educational psychology; and the psychology of religious experiences
Related Entries:
The James–Lange theory of emotion on p. 50 and the religious experience on p. 114

Jung, Carl
Dates: b. 1942
Nationality: Swiss
Related Areas:
Analytical psychology
Related Entries:
The foundation of Jungian psychiatry on pp. 112–13

Kagan, Jerome
Dates: b. 1929
Nationality: American
Related Areas:
The study of temperament
Related Entries:
The stability of temperament on p. 19

Kübler-Ross, Elizabeth
Dates: b. 1926
Nationality: Swiss
Related Areas:
The processes of death and mourning
Related Entries:
The denial, anger, bargaining, depression, acceptance model of mourning pp. 106–7

Lange, Carl
Dates: 1834–1900
Nationality: Danish
Related Areas:
The relationship between stimuli and emotions
Related Entries:
The James–Lange theory of emotion on p. 50

Layard, Richard (economist)
Dates: b. 1934
Nationality: British
Related Areas:
The development of "happiness economics"
Related Entries:
The factors that affect happiness on p. 100

LeDoux, Joseph E.
Dates: b. 1949
Nationality: American
Related Areas:
Neuroscience
Related Entries:
The mechanics of the emotional brain on pp. 12, 15, 17

Lorenz, Konrad
Dates: 1903–1989
Nationality: Austrian
Related Areas:
The study of animal behavior (known as ethology)
Related Entries:
The concept of "imprinting" on p. 68

MacLean, Paul
Dates: 1913–2007
Nationality: American
Related Areas:
Physiology, psychiatry, and brain research
Related Entries:
The mechanics of the emotional brain on p. 12

Matsumoto, David
Dates: b. 1959
Nationality: American
Related Areas:
Culture, emotion, social interaction, and communication
Related Entries:
Cultural differences in emotional expression on p. 37

Milgram, Stanley
Dates: 1933–1984
Nationality: American
Related Areas:
Social psychology
Related Entries:
Obedience and authority
on p. 146

Mill, John Stuart
Dates: 1806–1873
Nationality: British
Related Areas:
Political and economic theory,
utilitarianism
Related Entries:
The concept of higher and
lower pleasures on p. 145

Miller, Neal
Dates: 1909–2002
Nationality: American
Related Areas:
The autonomic nervous
system and classical
conditioning
Related Entries:
The frustration–aggression
hypothesis on p. 84

Pahnke, Walter
Dates: 1931–1971
Nationality: American
Related Areas:
Research into psychadelic
experience
Related Entries:
The religious experience
on p. 115

Pavlov, Ivan
Dates: 1849–1936
Nationality: Russian
Related Areas:
The psychology and
physiology of classical
conditioning
Related Entries:
Classical conditioning
on p. 124

Rozin, Paul
Dates: b. 1936
Nationality: American
Related Areas:
Preferences, likes and dislikes,
and disgust.
Related Entries:
The cultural evolution of
disgust on pp. 42–3

Seligman, Martin
Dates: b. 1942
Nationality: American
Related Areas:
Depression and abnormal
psychology
Related Entries:
Learned helplessness and
positive psychology on pp. 21,
101, 100–11

Veenhoven, Ruut
Dates: b. 1942
Nationality: Dutch
Related Areas:
The study of the social
conditions for human
happiness and the director
of the World Database of
Happiness
Related Entries:
The study of happiness
on p. 100

Zanjonc, Robert
Dates: 1923–2008
Nationality: Polish-American
Related Areas:
Social psychology
Related Entries:
The mere exposure effect
on p. 78

Zimbardo, Philip
Dates: b. 1933
Nationality: American
Related Areas:
Social psychology
Related Entries:
The Stanford prison
experiment on p. 145

index

references

In most cases throughout *This Book Has Feelings* direct references have been omitted in order to improve the ease of reading. The references and further reading given below are listed in the order that they appear within each chapter.

Chapter 1: Your Brain on Feelings

MacLean, P. D. (1990). *The Triune Brain in Evolution.* New York: Plenum.

LeDoux, J. E. (1998). *The Emotional Brain.* New York: Simon & Schuster.

Schiff, B. B. & Lamon, M. (1994). Inducing emotion by unilateral contraction of hand muscles, *Cortex*, 30, 247–254.

Izard, C. E. (1991). *The Psychology of Emotions.* New York: Plenum.

Kagan, J. (1994). *Galen's Prophecy: Temperament in Human Nature.* Colorado: Westview Press.

Kolb, B. & Whishaw, I. Q. (2001). *An Introduction to Brain and Behavior.* New York: Worth.

Descartes, R. (1637). *Discourse on Method* and *The Meditations.* (1968 edition) New York: Penguin.

Chalmers, D. (1995). Facing up to the problem of consciousness. *Journal of Consciousness Studies* 2(3): 200–19.

Chapter 2: The Evolution of Emotion

Darwin, C. (1859). *On the Origin of Species by Means of Natural Selection.* (2007 edition). New York: Cosimo.

Darwin, C. (1872). *The Expression of the Emotions in Man and Animals.* (2009 edition). New York: Penguin.

Ekman, P. (1972). Universals and cultural differences in facial expression of emotion, In Cole, J. (ed.) *Nebraska Symposium on Motivations.* Lincoln: University of Nebraska Press.

Ekman, P. & Friesen, W. V. (1971). Constants across culture in the face and emotion, *Journal of Personality and Social Psychology*, 17, 124–129.

Ekman, P. & Friesen, W. V. (1978). *Facial Action Coding System: A Technique for the Measurement of Facial Movement.* Palo Alto, CA: Consulting Psychologists Press.

Strack, F., Martin, L. L., & Strepper, S. (1988). Inhibiting and facilitating conditions of the human smile: a non-obtrusive test of the facial feedback hypothesis, *Journal of Personality and Social Psychology*, 54, 768–777.

Matsumoto, D., Takeuchi, S., Andayani, S., Kouznetsova, N., & Krupp, D. (1998). The contribution of individualism–collectivism to cross-national differences in display rules, *Asian Journal of Social Psychology*, 1, 147–165.

Sackheim, H. A., Gur, R. C., & Saucy, M. (1978). Emotions are expressed more intensely on the left side of the face, *Science*, 2, 434–436.

Goffman, E. & Best, J. (2005). *Interaction Ritual: Essays in Face-to-Face Behavior.* New Brunswick, NJ: Aldine Transaction.

Keltner, D. (1995). Signs of appeasement: evidence for the distinct displays of embarrassment, amusement, and shame, *Journal of Personality and Social Psychology*, 68, 441–454.

Rozin, P., Haidt, J., & McCauley, C. (1993). Disgust, in Lewis, M. & Haviland, J. (eds.) *Handbook of Emotions.* New York: Guilford Press.

Chapter 3: The Psychology of Emotion

Blaney, P. H. (1986). Affect and memory: a review, *Psychology Bulletin*, 99, 229–246.

Cannon, W. B. (1915). *Bodily Changes in Pain, Hunger, Fear and Rage: An Account of Recent Researches into the Function of Emotional Excitement.* New York: Appleton.

Eich, E. & Suedfeld, P. (1995). Autobiographical memory and affect under conditions of reduced stimulation. *Journal of Environmental Psychology*, 15, 321–326.

Ellsworth, P. C. (1994). William James and emotion: is a century of fame worth a century of misunderstanding? *Psychological Review*, (101)2, 222–229.

Forgas, J. P., Goldenberg, L., & Unkelbach, C. (2009). Can bad weather improve your memory? An unobtrusive field study of natural mood effects on real-life memory. *Journal of Experimental Social Psychology*, 54, 254–257.

Gilbert, D. T. & Wilson T. D. (2001). Miswanting: some problems in the forecasting of future affective states, in Forgas, J. P. (ed.) *Feeling and Thinking: The Role of Affect in Social Cognition.* Cambridge: Cambridge University Press.

Goleman, D. (1995). *Emotional Intelligence: Why it Can Matter More Than IQ.* London: Bloomsbury Publishing.

Halberstadt, J. B., Niedenthal, P. M., & Kushner, J. (2006). Resolution of lexical ambiguity by emotional state, *Psychological Science*, 6, 5, 278–282.

James, W. (1902). *The Varieties of Religious Experience: A Study in Human Nature.* (1985 edition). New York: Penguin.

James, W. (1884). What is an emotion? *Mind*, 9, 188–205.

Lazarus, R. S. (1982). Thoughts on the relations between emotion and cognition, *American Psychologist*, 37, 1019–1024.

Lewis, M. & Haviland, J. (eds.) *Handbook of Emotions.* New York: Guilford Press.

Loggia, M. L., Schweinhardt, P., Villemure, C., & Bushnell, M. C. (2008). Effects of psychological state on pain perception in the dental environment, *Journal of the Canadian Dental Association*, 74, 651–656.

McGinnies, E. (1949). Emotionality and perceptual defense, *Psychological Review*, 56, 4, 244–251.

Pavlov, I. P. (1927). *Conditioned Reflexes: An Investigation of the Physiological Activity of the Cerebral Cortex.* Anrep, G. G., (trans. 2003 edition) New York: Dover.

Stefanucci, J. K., & Storbeck, J. (under revision). Don't look down: emotional arousal elevates height perception.

Chapter 4: Love's Emotions
Averill, J. R. (1985). The social construction of emotion: with special reference to love, in Gergen, J. & Davis, K. E. (eds.), *The Social Construction of the Person.* New York: Springer Verlag.

Fisher, H. (2004). *Why We Love: The Nature and Chemistry of Romantic Love.* New York: Henry Holt.

Donaldson, Z. R. & Young, L. J. (2008). Oxytocin, vassopresin and the neurogenetics of sociality, *Science*, 7, 32, 900–904.

Lorenz, K. & Tinbergen, N. (1938). Taxis and instinctive action in the egg-retrieving behavior of the greylag goose, in Schiller, C. (ed. & trans.), *Instinctive Behavior: Development of a Modern Concept.* London: Methuen.

Bowlby, J. (1979). *The Making and Breaking of Affectional Bonds.* London: Tavistock.

Perrett, D., Lee, K., Penton-Voak, I., Burt, D. M., Rowland, Yoshikawa, S., Henzi, S. P., Castles, D., & Akamatsu, S. (1998). Effects of sexual dimorphism on facial attractiveness, *Nature*, 394, 884–887.

Previti, D. & Amato, P. R. (2003). Why stay married? Rewards, barriers, and marital stability, *Journal of Marriage and Family*, 63, 3, 561–573.

Gottman, J. M. (1998). Psychology and the study of marital processes, *Annual Review of Psychology*, 49, 169–197.

Murray, S. L. & Holmes, J. G. (1999). The (mental) ties that bind: cognitive structures that predict relationship resilience, *Journal of Personality and Social Psychology*, 82, 4, 563–581.

O'Rourke, N. & Cappeliez, P. (2005). Marital satisfaction and self-deception: reconstruction of relationship histories among older adults, *Social Behavior and Personality*, 33, 3, 273–282.

Zeitlow, P. H. & Sillars, A. L. (1988). Life-stage differences in communication during marital conflicts, *Journal of Social and Personal Relationships*, 5, 2, 223–245.

Dell, S. (1984). *Murder into Manslaughter.* Oxford: Oxford University Press.

Mooney, H. B. (1965). Pathologic jealousy and psychochemo-therapy, *British Journal of Psychiatry*, 111, 1023–1042

White, G. L. & Mullen, P. E. (1992). *Jealousy.* New York: Guildford.

Zajonc, R. (1984). On the primacy of effect, *American Psychologist*, 39, 117–123.

Chapter 5: The Angers
Bandura, A., Ross, D., & Ross, S. A. (1961). Transmission of aggression through imitation of aggressive models, *Journal of Abnormal and Social Psychology* 63, 575–582.

Bandura, A. (1965). Influence of models' reinforcement contingencies on the acquisition of imitative responses, *Journal of Personality and Social Psychology*, 1, 589–595.

158

Benson, H. (1984). *Beyond the Relaxation Response.* New York: Times Books.

Berkowitz, L. (1962). Violence in the mass media, in Berkowitz, L. *Aggression: A Social Psychological Analysis.* New York: McGraw-Hill.

Berkowitz, L. (1993). *Aggression: Its Causes, Consequences and Control.* New York: McGraw-Hill Higher Education.

Booth, J. & Mann, S. (2005). The Experience of workplace anger. *Leadership and Organisational Development Journal,* 27, 250–262.

Boyle, S. H., Jackson, W. G., & Suarez, E. C. (2007) Hostility, anger, and depression predict increases in C3 over a 10-year period, *Brain, Behavior, and Immunity,* 21, 6, 816–823.

Dollard, J., Doob, L. W., Miller, N. E., Mowrer, O. H., & Sears, R. R. (1939). *Frustration and Aggression.* New Haven: Yale University.

Holmes, T. H. & Rahe, R. H. (1967). The social readjustment rating scale, *Journal of Psychosomatic Research,* 12, 2, 213–218.

Kanner, A. D., Coyne, J. C., Schaefer, C., & Lazarus, R. S. (1981). Comparison of two modes of stress measurement: Daily hassles and uplifts versus major life events, *Journal of Behavioral Medicine,* 4, 1–39.

Kubzansky, L. D., Sparrow, D., Jackson, B., Cohen, S., Weiss, S. T. & Wright, R. J. (2006). Angry breathing: a prospective study of hostility and lung function in the normative aging study, *Thorax,* 61, 863–868.

Morgan, S. P. (1983). A research note on religion and morality: are religious people nice people? *Social Forces,* 61, 3, 683–692.

National Institute of Mental Health (1982). *Television and Behavior: Ten Years of Scientific Progress.* Washington, D.C.: U.S. Government Printing Office.

Parke, R. D., Berkowitz, L., Leyens, S. P., West. S., & Sebastien, R. S. (1977). Some effects of violent and nonviolent movies on the behaviour of juvenile delinquents, in Berkowitz, L. (ed.) *Advances in Experimental Social Psychology* (Volume 10). New York: Academic Press.

Phillips, D. P. (1986). Natural experiments on the effects of mass media violence on fatal aggression, in Berkowitz, L. (ed.) *Advances in Experimental Social Psychology* (Volume 19). New York: Academic Press.

Rahe, R. H., Mahan, J. L., Arthur, R.J. (1970). Prediction of near-future health change from subjects' preceding life changes, *Journal of Psychosomatic Research,* 14, 4, 401–406.

Schieman, S. (1999). Age and anger. *Journal of Health and Social Behavior,* 40, 273–289.

Signorelli, N. (2005). *Violence in the Media: A Reference Handbook.* Santa Barbara, CA: ABC-CLIO.

Chapter 6: Sadness and Joy

Beck, A. T., (1976). *Cognitive Therapy and the Emotional Disorders.* New York: Meridian.

Diener, E. (2000). Subjective well-being: the science of happiness and a proposal for a national index, *American Psychologist,* 55, 34–43.

Kubler-Ross, E. (1969) *On Death and Dying.* Austin: Touchstone.

Layard, R. (2005). *Happiness: Lessons From a New Science.* London: Penguin

New Economics Foundation (2009). *The Happy Planet Index 2.0.* www.happyplanetindex.org

Noleen-Hoeksema, S. & Morrow, J. (1991). A prospective study of depression and post-traumatic stress symptoms after a natural disaster: the 1989 Loma Prieta earthquake, *Journal of Personality and Social Psychology,* 61, 115–121.

Provine, R. (2001). *Laughter: A Scientific Investigation.* New York: Penguin.

Seligman, M. E. P. (2005). *Authentic Happiness.* London: Nicholas Brealey Publishing.

Seligman, M. E. P. (1974). Depression and learned helplessness, in Friedman, R. J. & Katz, M. (eds.) *The Psychology of Depression: Contemporary Theory and Research.* Washington, D.C.: Winston-Wiley.

Csikszentmihalyi, M. (1991). *Flow: The Psychology of Optimal Experience.* New York: Harper Perennial.

James, W. (1902). *The Varieties of Religious Experience: A Study in Human Nature.* (1985 edition). New York: Penguin.

Pahnke, W. N. (1966). Drugs and mysticism, *The International Journal of Parapsychology,* 3, 295–313.

Veenhoven, R. World Database of Happiness. www.worlddatabaseofhapiness.eur.nl.

Chapter 7: Fear and Excitement

Kessler, R. C., McGonagle, K. A., Zhao, S., Nelson, C. P., Hughes, M., Eshleman, S., Wittchen, H. U., & Kendler, K. S. (1994). Lifetime and 12-month prevalence of DSM-III-R psychiatric disorders in the United States: results form the national comorbidity survey, *Archives of General Psychiatry,* 51, 8–19.

Barlow, D. H. (2003) *Anxiety and its Disorder: The Nature and Treatment of Anxiety and Panic* (second edition). New York: Guildford Press.

Wegner, D. M., Schneider, D. J., Knutson, B., & McMahon, S. R. (1991). Polluting the stream of consciousness: the effect of thought suppression on the mind's environment, *Cognitive Therapy and Research,* 15, 141–152.

Pavlov, I. P. (1927). *Conditioned Reflexes: An Investigation of the Physiological Activity of the Cerebral Cortex.* Anrep, G. G., (trans. 2003 edition) New York: Dover.

Hall, C. S. (1953). A cognitive theory of dreams, *Journal of General Psychology*, 49, 273–282

Revonsuo, A. (2000). The reinterpretation of dreams: an evolutionary hypothesis of the function of dreaming, *Behavioral and Brain Sciences*, 23, 6.

LaBerge, S. (1990). *Lucid Dreaming.* New York: Ballantine.

Aaronson, E. (1999). *The Social Animal.* New York: Worth Freeman.

Zuckerman, M. (2006). *Sensation Seeking and Risky Behavior.* New York: American Psychological Association.

Lewis, C. S. (1950). *The Lion, the Witch and the Wardrobe.* London: Geoffrey Bles

Chapter 8: Emotions with Attitude
Holmes, D. S. (1984). Meditation and somatic arousal reduction, *American Psychologist*, 1–10.

Benson, H., Beary, J. F., & Carol, M. P. (1974). The relaxation response, *Psychiatry*, 37, 37–46.

Festinger, L. (1957). *A Theory of Cognitive Dissonance.* Stanford, CA: Stanford University Press.

Tracy, J. L. & Robins, R. W. (2007). Emerging insights into the nature and function of pride, *Current Directions in Psychological Science*, 16, 3, 147–150.

Nozick, R. (1974). *Anarchy, State, and Utopia.* New York : Basic Books.

Mill, J. S. (1863) *Utilitarianism.* Indianapolis: Hackett Publishing Company.

Milgram, S. (1963). Behavioral study of obedience, *Journal of Abnormal and Social Psychology*, 67, 371–378.

Zimbardo, P. (1971). The psychological power and pathology of imprisonment, statement prepared for the U.S. House of Representatives Committee on the Judiciary; subcommittee no. 3: Hearings on Prison Reform, San Francisco.

Frankl, V. E. (1956). *Man's Search for Meaning: An Introduction to Logotherapy.* New York: Pocket Books.

credits

Dr. Neil Scott is a registered occupational psychologist who works with organizations to identify and select the most appropriate staff. As well as writing widely on equal opportunities and assessment he is the author of countless psychological measures of ability, aptitude, and attitude including the "emotions and behaviors at work" scale. He has also produced questionnaires for the BBC's website.

Neil contributed Chapter 1: Your Brain on Feelings, Chapter 2: The Evolution of Emotion, Chapter 4: Love's Emotions, Chapter 6: Sadness and Joy, Chapter 7: Fear and Excitement, and Chapter 8: Emotions with Attitude.

Neil would like to thank James Evans and James Beattie at Quid for all their support and guidance, Matt Pagett for his illustrations, Sue Barker, Tim, Kate, Nev, Osbert, God, Leah, Nathan, and Daniel for most things. Most of all, love and thanks to my wife Sarah for support, ideas, patience, insight, and just being wonderful.

Dr. Sandi Mann is a senior lecturer in occupational psychology at the University of Central Lancashire. She has masters' degrees in developmental psychology and organizational psychology, as well as a doctorate in organizational psychology. Her background includes work in clinical psychology and journalism, and she has written several books. Her current research focuses on issues to do with emotional experience in the workplace, including stress and anger.

Sandi contributed Chapter 3: The Psychology of Emotion and Chapter 5: The Angers.

Image Credits

Image of Charles Darwin on page 30
© Public Domain | Library of Congress Prints and Photographs Division

Image of Paul Ekman on page 38
© Getty Images

Image of William James on page 50
© Getty Images

Image of Walter Cannon on page 50
© Bettmann | CORBIS

Image of Sigmund Freud on page 72
© CORBIS

Image of Martin Seligman on page 110
© Martin Seligman

Image of Carl Jung on page 122
© Hulton-Deutsch Collection | CORBIS

Image of Viktor E. Frankl on page 148
© Getty Images